MARCO  POLO

MON TENE GRO

HUNGARY

ROMANIA

Zagreb

CROATIA

Belgrade

BOSNIA AND
HERZEGOVINA

SERBIA

Sarajevo

BGR

MONTENEGRO

RKS

Podgorica

Adriatic
Sea

ALBA-
NIA

www.marco-polo.com

T0150568

THE TOURING APP

shows you the way...
including routes and offline maps!

GET MORE OUT OF YOUR MARCO POLO GUIDE

IT'S AS SIMPLE AS THIS

1 go.marco-polo.com/mon

2 download and discover

GO!

WORKS OFFLINE!

SYMBOLS

INSIDER TIP Insider-Tipp

★ Highlight

●●●● Best of …

🔆 Scenic view

☯ Responsible travel: fair
trade principles and the
environment respected

**PRICE CATEGORIES
HOTELS**

Expensive over 100 euros

Moderate 50–100 euros

Budget under 50 euros

The prices are for two persons
in a double room, including
breakfast, per night

**PRICE CATEGORIES
RESTAURANTS**

Expensive over 18 euros

Moderate 12–18 euros

Budget under 12 euros

Price of a meal comprising
three or four different dishes

MAPS IN THE GUIDEBOOK
(124 A1) Page numbers and coordinates refer to the road atlas
(0) Site/address located off the map. Coordinates are also given for places that are not marked on the road atlas A street map of Kotor can be found on p. 127.

(🔲 A–B 2–3) Refers to the removable pull-out map

INSIDE FRONT COVER:
The best Highlights

INSIDE BACK COVER:
Maps of Budva, Cetinje, Herceg Novi and Podgorica

The best MARCO POLO Insider Tips

Our top 15 Insider Tips

INSIDER **TIP** **Nudism in the Bojana Delta**

The country's longest nudist beach is located on the beautiful river island *Ada Bojana* → **p. 63**

INSIDER **TIP** **Feel at home**

Tamara Strugar has for many years welcomed guests to *Vila Tamara* in Ulcinj. From a garden filled with agaves and oleanders, you can enjoy the view of the beach and unforgettable sunsets → **p. 63**

INSIDER **TIP** **Fresh air, good food**

After visiting the famous Ostrog Monastery, the *Koliba Bogetići* Motel is the perfect place to return to earthly spheres out in the fresh air → **p. 79**

INSIDER **TIP** **"The Boat" for real**

Not in the ocean, but at the museum – inside the Yugoslavian submarine *Heroj*, you are still guaranteed claustrophobia and intrigue → **p. 45**

INSIDER **TIP** **On a zipline above the canyon**

At Đurđevića Tara Bridge, you will overcome your vertigo! With the *Redrockzipline* you race 150 m/492 ft high above the canyon with the meandering river below → **p. 83**

INSIDER **TIP** **Rock sounds on the beach**

Britons rate the *Sea Dance Festival* at Jaz Beach near Budva among the best music events in Europe. For many, it's still unknown and is regarded as an insider tip → **p. 108**

INSIDER **TIP** **No frills**

The restaurant *Konoba* in Kolašin is a rustic wooden hut with hearty cuisine and low prices → **p. 88**

INSIDER **TIP** **Angelic voices in the fjord**

Klape are male a capella choirs that sing slow ballads. The best of them perform at the *festival of male choirs* held in Perast in August → **p. 108**

INSIDER TIP Ruins with a view

Montenegro's rulers once resided in Žabljak on Lake Skadar. There is a splendid view far across the landscape from the *castle ruins* → **p. 75**

INSIDER TIP Balkans go vegetarian

It's true that meat is very popular in the Balkans. But you will increasingly find excellent vegetarian alternatives – for instance, at *Peter's Pie and Coffee.* And the restaurant is on the attractive promenade in Herceg Novi! → **p. 36**

INSIDER TIP Reach for the sky

Easy hikes aren't enough for you? The challenging *Peaks of the Balkans Trail* takes you high into the Prokletije Mountains (photo left) → **p. 89**

INSIDER TIP River canyon motel

It's hard to believe that it's so peaceful here: the small *Motel Tara MB* is located next to the impressive bridge over the Tara River Canyon. And the food is also good → **p. 83**

INSIDER TIP A touch of Saint Tropez

The feel of southern France: the small village of *Rose* consists of a few stone houses with the sea right on the doorstep. The picturesque village has become a hub for artists and film stars from Belgrade who like to spend their holidays in the shade of the olive trees (photo below) → **p. 47**

INSIDER TIP Aroma therapy

Breathe in, browse around and taste – every morning beguiling fragrances waft over Bar when the *farmers' market* displays the wealth of Mediterranean nature → **p. 51**

INSIDER TIP Stones of remembrance

The *Jewish cemetery* in Kotor is the only one of its kind in Montenegro. It is a silent witness to the exodus of Spanish Jews in the Middle Ages who found their new home in this city. A pebble placed on a tombstone honours the deceased → **p. 40**

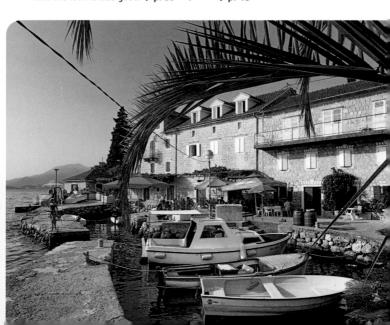

BEST OF ...

GREAT PLACES FOR FREE
Discover new places and save money

● *Scenic road instead of a tunnel*

The 2.50 euros that you will have to pay if you drive through the Sozina Tunnel from Lake Skadar to the Montenegrin coast are admittedly not much. But: the alternative route via the winding road from Virpazar on the Adriatic near Petrovac is free and offers panoramic vistas → p. 50

● *Montenegro's up-and-coming artists*

This is the place to discover new talent! The *Gallery Josip Bepo Benković* in Herceg Novi exhibits work by young Montenegrin artists. You don't have to pay to have a look at them → p. 35

● *Collect herbs*

Mint, thyme, rocket and nettles – all of the fragrant herbs of Montenegro are on sale at the country's markets. But it is much more fun to pick them yourself! So just head off to the hinterland of Lake Skadar and get away from the main roads! The herbs grow wild near *Virpaza* for example → p. 75

● *A must – walking across a bridge*

Even if you're not a fan of adventures like riding the zipline or rafting, you should definitely visit the Tara Canyon. The walk across *Đurđevića Tara Bridge* and fantastic views are entirely free of charge → p. 83

● *Free fortress in Budva*

You can visit the *Citadel* in the Adriatic town free of charge – and in summer the open-air concerts are a bonus → p. 53

● *Free bench at the beach*

A sun lounger on the beach in *Petrovac na Moru* costs 10 euros; a place on one of the lovely old benches on the promenade is completely gratis. You will still have the sand and sea right in front of you and trees to provide shade (photo) → p. 58

●●●●● Dots in guidebook refer to "Best of ..." tips

● *Coffee tradition*

No day is complete without a mocha in Montenegro, no matter if it is in the morning, at midday or in the evening. Coffee is served in small cups with a glass of water. Try a coffee in the traditional *patisserie Karađuzović* in Stari Bar. Also served with delicious Baklava → **p. 53**

● *Monument on the summit*

The Montenegrins revere their national heroes with great fervour and they have placed a colossal monument to the greatest on one of the highest mountains in the country. The poet Prince Njegoš has found his final resting place in the *mausoleum,* with spectacular views, on the Jezerski vrh summit on Mount Lovćen (photo) → **p. 68**

● *Lamb, baked over hot coals*

When you are in Podgorica, you have to sample a traditional Montenegrin delicacy at the restaurant *Kužina*: juicy lamb baked in a ceramic dish over an open fire. The secret: even the ceramic lid *sač* is covered with hot coals → **p. 71**

● *Our daily bread*

Those who want to buy bread in Montenegro must generally make do with rather tasteless loaves subsided by the state and known as "people's bread". Many locals prefer to bake their own bread. Especially the fresh bread that the farmers' wives in the north bake is pure bliss! You have the opportunity to enjoy it as a visitor at the *Autocamp Razvršje* camping site where the owner's mother bakes her own bread → **p. 80**

● *An old town like a museum*

The fate of the small country has repeatedly been determined by European powers. You can experience the diversity of the cultural heritage on a tour of the impressive *old town* of Kotor with its dignified churches and palaces → **p. 40**

● *Unspoilt Adriatic coast? Where?*

You can get to know the real Adriatic coast on the *Luštica* Peninsula. Okay, property investors have also tried their luck here. But a big part of this development over 18 mi^2 is still wonderfully unspoilt: old stone houses, endless olive grows and secluded bays and beaches! → **p. 47**

ONLY IN

BEST OF ...

● **Orthodox sanctuary, carved out of rock**
The Metropolitan Bishop of Herzegovina had the *Ostrog* Monastery built into the cliffs as a place of refuge from the Turks. If you seek shelter from the rain here, you will find peace in the tranquil rooms and fascinating frescoes on stone (photo) → p. 79

● **Brave raindrops on the sand**
Walking barefoot along the beach and having your feet massaged by the wet sand – the mild climate of the Adriatic makes it possible for you to do this with or without an umbrella; try it on the *Grand Beach* in Ulcinj → p. 62

● **Art, ultra-modern please**
Most Montenegrin artists' have a style that is in character with their country: full of power, energy and colour. That makes it impossible to think of the rain outside! The *Centar savremene umjetnosti* in Podgorica displays contemporary art → p. 70

● **Silver screen dreams**
Enjoy Montenegro's lively cinematic landscape on a rainy evening. The *Kino Kultura* in Podgorica shows foreign films in their original language. The film director Emir Kusturica is the owner of the venerable *Hotel Aurora* in Herceg Novi. Watching the classics in the hotel's impressive cinema is nicer than ever before → pp. 71, 38

● **Vive le sport!**
At *Bijela* you can test your stamina in the power sports facilities playing tennis, judo or boxing – everything is indoor. At the diving course, it doesn't matter whether it's raining → p. 39

● **Museum to shellbacks**
The area around the Bay of Kotor is the birthplace of many famous captains who braved the wind and weather on the high seas. You can be inspired by their feats in the *Maritime Museum* in Kotor → p. 40

RAIN

RELAX AND CHILL OUT
Take it easy and spoil yourself

● *Tranquil cloister at the end of the world*
A day on God's soil: take a boat ride to *Beška Island* where a handful
of nuns lead a life of seclusion. In this place you will be able to find
peace of mind and think over all you have experienced on your trip in
the small church or by just looking at the wild pomegranates → **p. 73**

● *Sea breeze and massage*
The changing winds and the long, pristine bay in Buljarica are a tonic
for the lungs and the owner of the small *Savojo Hotel* will take care
of any back pains with a massage on the beach → **p. 60**

● *Luxurious oasis of relaxation*
Take in the view of the mountains around the Bay of Kotor from the
swimming pool, enjoy a massage or just relax while the waves lap
against the yachts in the sea only a few metres away – the *Yacht Club
Pool* in Tivat offers luxury relaxation (photo) → **p. 46**

● *Broom in bloom on the coast*
When the broom is in bloom at the end of May, the coast road of
the Adriatic meanders through a sea of yellow. Find a pleasant spot
on the peaceful bay of *Dobra Voda*, lay down on your picnic blanket
and take in the enchanting sight → **p. 52**

● *Wellness with tradition*
The team of doctors and physiotherapists in the *Institut Igalo* have
been taking care of their guests for more than six decades. Mud
packs and aromatherapy are
just two of the items
on offer → **p. 39**

● *Wine, dine and chillax*
This restaurant terrace
is stylish and relaxing
at the same time.
And those breath-
taking views! The
Olive is directly
opposite charming
Sv. Stefan island.
Here, you will
completely forget
the rest of the
world → **p. 57**

INTRODUCTION

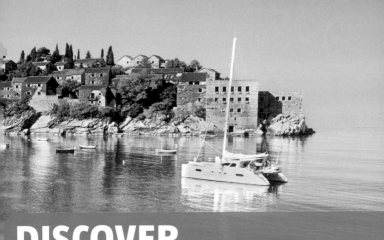

DISCOVER MONTENEGRO!

Only a few hours flying time from London, Edinburgh or Dublin lies a little holiday paradise with a *variety of landscapes* and sites that bear witness to an *eventful history*: Montenegro, the land of the Black Mountain (Monte Negro), the land of heroes and pirates that drove the Turks out of the mountains and raided Venetian ships in the Middle Ages, is still relatively unknown. Montenegro's coastal strip is not even 300 km/186 mi long and swimmers have only *70 km/43.5 mi of beach* available for their pleasure; the other half of the country is dominated by the *mountains* at an altitude of over 1,000 m/3,281 ft above sea level. Raging rivers wind their way through the deep canyons of the Durmitor and Bjelasica mountain ranges. Snow-covered peaks are reflected in tiny alpine lakes. The Montenegrins have buried their most famous poet Petar II Petrović Njegoš on one of the countless *mountain ranges*, the Lovćen, and from his burial site there are panoramic views all the way to Bosnia, Croatia, Albania and – on a clear day – to Italy.

The distance between the most westerly and easterly points in Montenegro is a mere 176 km/109 mi and the country measures only 200 km/124 mi from north to south. However, where do you have so much to see and experience in such a small area?

The railway line between Belgrade and Bar is one of the most spectacular in the Balkans

After the Grand Canyon, the *Tara River Canyon* in the north-west of the country is the deepest in the world and one of the last primeval forests in Europe lies hidden in the highlands in the *Biogradska Gora National Park*. More birds nest on *Lake Skadar* than on any other in Europe and the *only fjord in the Mediterranean* lies beneath almost perpendicular rock faces between the towns of Herceg Novi and Kotor. Nowhere else on the eastern Adriatic are there more beautiful sandy beaches than between Bar and Ulcinj. The *idyllic bays* hidden behind rocks and lined with pines, cypresses and olive trees are typical of Montenegro's coastline. A stroll through the flower town of Herceg Novi, the seafaring hamlet of Perast or across the picturesque hotel island of Sv. Stefan will take you back to the *heyday of European*

> **Rarely can one experience so much in such a small area**

Approx. 1200 BC
Illyrians settle in the region around Lake Skadar

2nd century BC
The Roman Empire pushes back the Illyrians

7th century AD
Slavs force their way into the Roman province of Duklja. The Montenegrin principality of Zeta is established under Byzantine rule

15th–18th century
Venetian rule of the coastal towns of Kotor, Ulcinj, Budva and Bar

1815–1918
The Habsburg Empire controls sections of the coastline

architecture. The pedestrian area of the old town of Kotor reveals an architectural melange of Venetian Baroque buildings and Austro-Hungarian town houses. *Centuries-old Orthodox monasteries* are tucked away further inland.

The Montenegrins defend the country's multicultural spirit, which continued to flourish here after the collapse of Josip Broz Tito's Socialist Yugoslavia, with great fervour. Croats, Serbs, Albanians, Roma and Muslims have lived alongside each other for centuries – and both the government and opposition of the small republic stress the virtue of this tolerance in their efforts to accede to the European Union. The Montenegrins have no doubt that their country's roots can be found deep in Europe: you will discover *traces of the rich history* of this small country wherever you go. In Cetinje, the old embassy buildings recall the time when the nine daughters of Tsar Nicholas I married into the major courts of Europe and the

> **The Montenegrins defend their multicultural spirit with great élan**

wily diplomat was known as the "father-in-law of Europe". Well before that, noble families from Venice to Petersburg had invited Montenegrin artists and captains into their employ. And, the *European roots* sink even deeper: Greeks, Illyrians and Romans settled in the area south of Dubrovnik before the Roman Empire divided its territory at the end of the 4th century.

It was not until the 1960s that the small country with a rich cultural diversity was discovered as a *holiday destination*. And then things really took off for Montenegro

1878
The Congress of Berlin recognises Montenegro as a sovereign, independent state

1918
Independence ends with defeat in the First World War. Montenegro becomes part of the new Kingdom of Serbs, Croats and Slovenes

Second World War
Italian troops occupy Montenegro in 1941. Under the leadership of Milovan Đilas, Montenegrin partisans join Tito's revolt against the occupation. Montenegro is liberated in 1944

that had always brought up the rear in economic terms among the six Yugoslav constituent states. Anybody who had a spare bed rented it to a tourist. Hotels with "beguiling socialist charm" sprang up everywhere. Sv. Stefan, the fishing island carved out of stone, became an exclusive holiday location for celebrities such as Sophia Loren and Michael Douglas. However, the *Yugoslavian war* in the 1990s crippled the entire economy once again. Although there was no action in the country itself, Montenegro suffered from the uncertain political situation in the Balkans: the once popular holiday destination for Europeans fell out of favour. Hotels and guesthouses fell into disrepair and poverty once again hit the country. Primarily, many young university graduates went abroad to find work.

> **Montenegro has remained a country for dreamers and explorers**

Since then, Montenegrins hold out great hope for a *membership in the European Union*. Many politicians felt that the confederation with Serbia was an obstacle on Montenegro's path into the European Union. Milo Đukanovič, who was president from 1998 to 2002 and Prime Minister several times after that, did everything he could to promote secession. He introduced *the euro as the country's currency* in 2002 and established borders within the state of Serbia-Montenegro. A narrow majority (55 per cent) voted for independence from Serbia in a referendum.

Isn't that a long time ago? Yes and no: even years after the secession the turbulence has not entirely subsided. Almost 30 per cent of the population still define themselves as Serbian. The feeling of solidarity is anchored in history; many Montenegrins regard *Serbia* and the former Yugoslavia as their second home. The common language and history create a lasting relationship. However, despite everything Montenegro will certainly not give up its *independence* again that many are very proud of.

For a long time Montenegro struggled with the economic challenges that came with the *transition from socialism to capitalism*. The privatisation of state companies was often a failure, and the result was high unemployment. For several years there has been a gradual upswing; the unemployment rate fell in 2018 to 17 per cent, while average salaries rose to almost 800 euros gross. The economic growth is projected

1992
Proclamation of the Federal Republic of Yugoslavia, consisting of Serbia and Montenegro

2006
Montenegro withdraws from the Serbia-Montenegro confederation

2012
After becoming a candidate for European Union accession in 2010, the European Union decides to start accession negotiations with Montenegro

2017
At the NATO Summit in Brussels, Montenegro becomes a new member of the alliance – against protests from Serbia and Russia.

Hot spot for well-heeled visitors to the Adriatic: the luxurious Porto Montenegro in Tivat

at 3 per cent. The introduction of the euro attracted many *foreign investors* to the country that mainly invested in the hotel industry. Many luxury resorts, marinas and golf courses are being built mainly along the coast. Chinese companies are building Montenegro's first motorway. By 2020, the first 41 km/24.9 mi around the capital shall open.

Irrespective of all the commercial and political developments, Montenegro is still a place for dreamers and explorers. *"Wild Beauty"* is the country's advertising slogan to attract tourists, and you can still find *unspoiled countryside* in some places. The hospitality of the 643,000 Montenegrins is legendary. "The guest is king" is the motto in Montenegro, and your hosts will welcome you with *sincerity and warmth*.

Those who are lucky enough to be on the spot for the *slava family festival* are naturally invited. The celebration lasts up to three days and includes dancing, singing and lots of laughter. That's another endearing quality of

The Montenegrins' hospitality is proverbial

Montenegrins: they *like to laugh*, even at themselves. Friendships made mainly in the small guesthouses and hotels are long-lasting, and many guests regularly return. They have been impressed by the *friendly atmosphere* in their holiday home – enjoying a glass of wine on the veranda in the evening with figs, olives and some cheese, relaxed conversations with hosts – these experiences create wonderful holiday memories.

WHAT'S HOT

1 Freshly brewed

Coffee addicts Young Montenegrins' coffee craze is for classic filter coffee. *Dojčkafa* ("German coffee") is the country's most popular drink. It's compulsory, especially in Njegoševa street in Podgorica, where there are numerous bars and clubs like *Kafić Berlin (Njegoševa 24 | tel. 020 23 43 67 | short.travel/mon12)*.

Rustic living

Eco villages Rustic exteriors with comfortable interiors – that's typical of the houses in the *etno-* or *eko-selos* of mountain regions. Traditionally built from stone and wood, they resemble the local huts. But they're much more inviting with a bathroom, kitchen and solid furnishings. Regional organic food is served. In the mountain village of *Brezna (www.facebook.com/etno.selo)* near Plužine, guests plunge straight from the sauna into the mini-pool at an altitude of 1,000 m/3,281 ft. Go self-sufficient with nature's harvest – that's possible in *Komnenovo etno selo (www.kuladamjanova.com)* in Vojno Selo near Plav: the trout jump in the lake right outside the door!

2

3 Food to go

Street food tastes best In Montenegro, street food is hugely popular. "That was always a Balkan tradition", you will say. True. But the Western craze has made it even more popular. "Chippy" sounds so authentic, doesn't it? Whatever it's called – there is simply, delicious grilled food to go, e.g. in the *Tanjga Family Restaurant (Suranj bb | on E65 near the big roundabout)* in Kotor. The *Home of Gyros (Novembra 29)* in Budva is no culinary Olympus, but it has "street cred".

Green gold

All about olives Young Montenegrins discover their cultural heritage: forgotten olive groves are revived, and the olives are harvested by hand and processed in ancient stoneground mills. The product is premium quality cold-pressed olive oil. And that's a reason to celebrate! In July, the *maslinarke*, women olive farmers of the association *Boka (www. maslinaboka.org)* in Tivat host the *Day of the Olive*. In Stari Bar, where the *Olive Oil Association* also has its headquarters *(www.oliveoilmontene gro.me)*, the Maslinijada olive festival is after the harvest in November. A small gem and authentic and rich source of olive oil products is *Olive Ponte (Rr Ymer Prizreni | next to Restaurant Ponto | www.oliveponte.com)* in Ulcinj. Almir Kolari sells oil, soaps and even furniture.

4

Art revival

New galleries The Russian gallery owner Marat Guelman is really mixing up the country's art scene. His *Dukley European Art Community (dukleyart. me)* gives Montenegrin artists the chance to display their artwork with a wide range of exhibition spaces. In Kotor, Guelman emphasises the inspirational effect of industrial charm: with studios and exhibition rooms, he brings new life to the former shipyard *Jugooceanija (Njegoševa bb)*. In Cetinje, he plans to help the Montenegrin star artist Marina Abramović transform the factory Obod into an art centre. After a promising start, the project *Macco* has now run out of impetus. Can Guelman revive it from its long slumber?

5

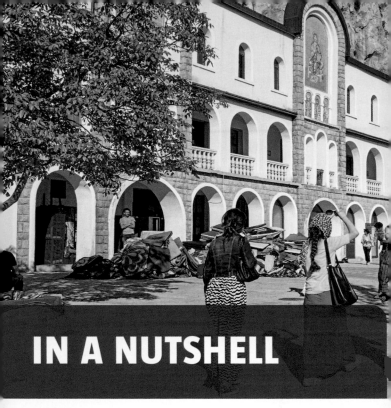

IN A NUTSHELL

TALLEST MEN, SMALL COUNTRY

They say size doesn't always matter in life. And even if it did, Montenegro couldn't grumble, as it's catered for at both ends of the scale. According to population size (about 643,000) the country isn't even an "also ran" in the international rankings – it features even lower down the list at number 168. But Montenegro is still ahead of heavyweights like Cape Verde, Kiribati and the Isle of Man.

Anyway, a good look is much more important than high numbers: and that's certainly true here. Montenegrin men are the tallest in the world, while the Montenegrin women are only beaten by the Dutch. It's not clear whether it's down to the mountain- and sea air, the *ćevapčići* meat or the urge to be nearer to the sky!

CRNA GORA

Okay, that's quite a lot of consonants together. But somehow you can pronounce it – try "Tsrna Gora". It means "Black Mountain" or simply "Montenegro". The Venetians coined the name in the Middle Ages when they conquered Kotor, Budva and Ulcinj. In the Slavic version *gora* can mean "mountain" as well as "forest" or "wood". When you see how the low afternoon sun shines on the pine forests of the Durmitor Mountains, you will understand why the Montenegrins tend to translate the name of their country as "Black Forest".

Photo: Ostrog Monastery

Strong women, tallest men, admiring Russians and a great domain name – it's all possible in Montenegro!

HEROISM AND HONOUR

"I don't want to be a monument – the pigeons only drop on it." This is how Austria's football idol Toni Polster summarized the popular idea that monuments are boring! (Of course, he used slightly less polite language to describe the pigeons). Nonetheless, in Montenegro, people love monuments commemorating all kinds of things – usually, brave fighters, war heroes and poets and almost always men. The motto is *Cojstvo i junaštvo* or "honour and heroism". Numerous legends were created especially in the battle against Turkish rule, for instance, about the untamed mountain princes who feared no enemies. During this era the population was divided into clans. Until today, almost all locals know which clan *(pleme)* and fraternity *(bratstvo)* they belong to. It could come in handy again.

WOMEN RARELY INDULGE

Don't remind the locals, if you want to

avoid friction: even well into the 1960s, in many towns in Montenegro a woman walked several steps behind her husband as a mark of respect. Things have radically changed. Now, many prominent businesswomen and female politicians and women appear self-confident and self-determined – even if society still follows patriarchal rules. In other words: usually, in the end the men still have a say.

A crazy relic of long and rightly forgotten times are the *virginas,* or the "third sex". In some remote mountain villages like Tušine and Šavnik they still exist: women, who dress and behave like men, as they have to manage the house and farm because no sons were born in the family.

B EAUTY FADES, LAND HOLDS VALUE

Montenegro hadn't even been independent for two years when foreigners were legally permitted to purchase land. Many people took advantage and invested in all the best plots. Prices sky-rocketed and locals who owned land on the Adriatic benefitted when their previously modest estates increased in value. Montenegro partly gave up control of the country's best real estate. Many hotels and other unattractive complexes were developed along the coast that now look out of place. Some access paths to beaches were blocked. On the other hand, the flood of foreign investment also brought welcome capital to the country that helped Montenegro with its economic expansion. Fortunately, now the frenetic building boom has slowed down slightly.

T HERE IS ONLY ONE PETAR NJEGOŠ!

Never heard of this Montenegrin writer? You're not alone. But you should remember this unique name: Petar II Petrović

Njegoš (1813–51), – aka the "poet prince". He could not only create beautiful rhymes, but he was also one of the most multifacetted personalities in the history of this tiny state.

As a bishop and prince he reformed the outdated political system with its antiquated clan structures and by doing so brought Montenegro closer to Europe. Because that wasn't enough, he honoured all Southern Slavic literature with his masterpiece "The Mountain Wreath" *(Gorski Vjenac)* that was required reading in the Balkans until the 1990s. The subject (how could it be otherwise?) is the heroic struggle of his predecessor Danilo I to liberate the country from the Turks and – the other side of the coin – the murder of thousands of Islam converts. Njegoš wrote down many of the verses, which have their roots in popular poetry, for the first time and in so doing significantly brought forward the standardisation of the written language. An extract: "When things go well 'tis easy to be good/in suffering one learns who the real hero is". Wise words.

Because his words set monuments, he was built a stone memorial – the largest in the land: the sizeable mausoleum on Lovćen, "Montenegro's Olympus".

A LL IN EUROS, OKAY?

I'm sorry? Montenegro is not in the EU and still has the euro? During the 1960s after guest workers had begun to bring back their hard-earned German marks to Yugoslavia, German money became a parallel currency to the dinar. In 2000, Montenegro without further ado established the German mark as the only means of payment. This was a first sign of Montenegrin independence from Serbia six years later. The German Bundesbank reacted calmly at the time. Then, the German mark became the

Monumental resting place for the poet prince: Njegoš Mausoleum on Mount Lovćen

euro. That was it. Only Montenegro is naturally not allowed to print money itself or participate in any decisions. The cash must be procured from the "genuine" euro zone. The country still has a stable currency. Pretty smart, don't you think?

THE RUSSIANS ARE HERE

If you think you can hear Russian everywhere in Montenegro, that's because Russian is spoken everywhere in Montenegro. Many Russians have made the country their second home. Firstly, this is because of history because during the wars against the Turks in the 19th century the Tsar's soldiers fought side by side

with the locals who never forgot that. In tiny Montenegro, Russians feel welcome – they are by far the largest tourist group and major investors and owners of real estate. More than 10,000 Russians live in Budva alone.

There are also practical benefits: Montenegro also uses the Cyrillic alphabet like Russia and although it is not a member of the EU, it is a good bridge to Western Europe.

Of course, this still doesn't mean that Russian influences are enthusiastically accepted. If you try to start speaking Russian, you may well be ignored. But this tends to be the exception.

Since the annexation of the Crimea in Ukraine and Montenegro's NATO

After the storm is before the storm in the Durmitor Mountains in the north

membership – which was highly controversial in the country – political relations have considerably cooled off. But the flow of tourists from "Mother Russia" continues: in 2017, twice as many Russians arrived as a decade earlier, i.e. over 300,000 – more than a quarter of all overnight stays by foreign visitors.

THE CALM AFTER THE STORM

In spring and late autumn the weather can be cold and wet. The sunny and dry half-year in summer is heralded by rainy days that can be quite stormy: the heavens open and torrents of water stream down the steeply sloping streets and gush into the drains. The waves on the Adriatic coast are dramatic and the clouds turn black. However, the wet and miserable weather is usually over before you know it. Afterwards, the plants and trees are wonderfully fragrant and the air is sharp and clear as the sun shines again. What was all the fuss about? But five minutes later, the bad weather can start all over again. It can get particularly dramatic in the mountainous north.

DO YOU SPEAK SERBO-MONTENEGRIN?

It was a really close result: before the referendum about independence from

Serbia, it was decided that turnout should be at least 50 per cent and there must be a vote of at least 55 per cent. Voter turnout was then a massive 86 per cent, but the pro-independence vote was exactly 55.49 per cent. It was right on target. However, this also means that plenty of people wanted to remain part of Serbia. Somehow, things were quite comfortable with the big brother. Nevertheless, after the vote for independence, Montenegrin was constitutionally introduced as the official language. However, many people still used Serbian as usual as their colloquial language. Recent surveys show the ratio is still about fifty-fifty. Serbian-speaking people demand more state funding because in their view the government clearly gives privileges to Montenegrin.

The good news is that the differences between the two languages are relatively minimal. For example, the Montenegrin word for river is *rijeka* and the Serbian equivalent is *reka*; world is *svijet* instead of *svet*, and morning is *sjutra* instead of *sutra*. Important phrases like *dobar dan* (hello) and *hvala* (thank you) are identical.

The minority 5 per cent of Albanians in the country have it even easier. In the south and north-east, where the Albanians live, bilingualism is incorporated in law.

SAINT'S DAY FESTIVAL

Every orthodox family has a patron saint. Saint's days call for a celebration: *Slava* lasts for several days and has been celebrated every year for centuries. It is probably the most important family festival in Montenegro. Its origins date from the old Slavic and pre-Christian tradition. People spend days preparing ritual food, cleaning the house, until the priest finally appears on saint's day and gives his blessing. The festival starts and the party continues with dancing and lengthy celebrations. Every monastery also has its own patron saint, for example Ostrog Monastery, which is hewn into the rock, celebrates St Vasilije on 12 May.

MONTENEGRO'S DOMAINS

Obviously, nobody in Montenegro thought of cool Internet addresses when the country declared its independence from Serbia in 2006. But when independence was declared, suddenly a country code was needed or a "top level domain" like .ch for Switzerland. The abbreviation .me was still available, so it was adopted. Since 2007, Montenegrin websites end with these letters. Everybody can give a domain name an ending – for example, .uk, .ch- or .me-, regardless of the country of residence. This is why .me now also represents a number of web addresses from the US state of Maine and the *Middle East*. But the fun started when marketing experts first noticed the ending. The ending "me" turns the website into an invitation: e.g. *www.follow.me* or *www.forgive.me* are two of the most obvious examples. Major companies also acquired the name: if you type in *mercedes.me* or *facebook.me*, you are directed to the company's main website. In 2012, in the US an advertising campaign was aired with the slogan, "You're not a company, but a person". Viewers were persuaded to use .me for their private websites instead of .com. About half of the .me web addresses were allocated in the US. Initially, the Montenegrin government managed the domains and earned 17 million euros in a decade. Typical Montenegro – a small country that's made it big!

FOOD & DRINK

The country might be small but the variety of culinary delights is enormous! Most of it comes from Montenegro's abundant natural resources. Contented cows graze on the mountain slopes and in the valleys. Mushrooms and wild herbs, such as mint and thyme, grow off the main highways. There are olive groves and avenues of fig trees, and vegetables out of the garden in summer. For the past few years, there has been a noticeable trend of **sustainable food culture** in Montenegro. There are also several hundred officially certified organic farmers and the number is growing every year. In the mountains everything grows naturally and olive and fig trees have grown in coastal region for centuries. Farmers can only sell their *locally grown products* at markets or fairs, as the large supermarkets have no space for them. Local products are also sold by street vendors – not always, but often for very fair prices. If restaurants offer ham and cheese from the region, you can assume that these are produced by local mountain farmers.

Almost all restaurants on the coast and many bars serve you **sea fish** – grilled *(na žaru)*, boiled *(lešo)* or in a casserole *(brodeto)*. You can also savour mussels in white wine *(mušule buzara)* or stuffed squid *(punjeni lignji)*. In the Middle Ages, the Venetians not only left architectural traces in Montenegro, but also brought their culinary arts with them. Fine *Italian cuisine* still influences the gastronomy of the coastal region in

Fresh from nature to the dish: sea, lakes and rivers, fields, meadows and pastures provide the ingredients for Montenegro's rich cuisine

pasta and fish recipes. Pasta dishes and pizza are also available as fast food in the highlands of the north.

Montenegro's second major culinary district is located between the coast and the mountains and characterised by the *wealth of fish in Lake Skadar*. This is where you will find eel, carp and bleak on your plate – grilled, dried, boiled, smoked or pan-fried. You can also enjoy many of these *fish specialities* in the restaurants in the capital city, Podgorica. With the possible exception of trout

(pastrmka) and carp, the realm of fish in the frying pan or pot ends in Podgorica. *Meat* takes over – and the cooking in the higher regions around Kolašin, Žabljak and Nikšić is correspondingly hearty. Everything the pastures and farms produce finds its way to the plate – *high-quality natural ingredients* that will not only appeal to fans of organic food. You should try lamb that is baked under a *sač*, a large metal or ceramic bell shaped lid covered with ashes and live coals. The best place to enjoy

LOCAL SPECIALITIES

balšića tava – strips of veal topped with a sauce of eggs, milk and cream
bokeljski brodet – fish stew with sprats, anchovies or similar fish simmered in a broth of onions, white wine, parsley, olive oil and garlic
crni rižot – risotto coloured black by squid ink
imam bajeldi – fried aubergine with a tomato, garlic and onion mixture
jagnjetina u mlijeku – lamb cooked in milk and then browned
kačamak – cheesy Montenegrin polenta; made with corn flour like its Italian counterpart
kajmak – fresh creamy cheese similar to clotted cream (photo left)
krap u tavu – carp cooked in a pan and served with prunes, apples and quince

Krstač – full-bodied, dry white wine
Nikšićko pivo – *the* Montenegrin beer
njeguška šnicla – breaded pork escalope stuffed with *kajmak*, ham and sheep milk cheese
paštrovski makaruli – noodles that are made with whole wheat flour served with olive oil and cheese preserved in brine
pastrmka u kiselom mlijeku – trout in yogurt; eaten cold
priganice – fried pastry served with honey, similar to a donut
riblja juha – fish soup (photo right)
sir u ulju – sheep milk cheese preserved in olive oil
Vranac Pro Corde – the best Montenegrin red wine; is said to be good for the heart

this is in a traditional round wooden hut (*savardak*). The **njeguški pršut** (air dried ham) and **njeguški sir**, which is similar to ricotta, come from the village Njeguši, between Cetinje and Kotor. They are offered in small family-run **konobas** (taverns) where they are served with a thick slice of bread that each family bakes in a wood-burning stove following its own recipe and a glass of *medovina* (old Slavic honey drink) and you will be able to relax and enjoy a unique view of the Lovćen Mountains. Another special treat is the fresh **goat's cheese** *mladi kozji sir*. The best is produced in the Kolašin region in the north-east.

No meal in Montenegro would be complete without **bread**. The *narodni hleb* is the traditional loaf: all bakeries are required to have a stock of this so-called "people's bread", which is subsidised by the state and only costs around 0.50 euros. However, the bread is somewhat bland. This is made up for by the delicious traditional *turnovers (pita)*: sheets of *jufka* pastry filled with cheese *(sirnica)*, spinach *(zeljanica)* or meat *(burek)* and accompanied by a glass of yogurt. Typical types of Balkan fast-food are *ćevapčići*, spicy meat rolls served with chips and raw onions, and *pljeskavica* (hamburger). You can buy them at kiosks wherever you are in the country.

Sometime a *salad* is all you will need on a hot summer day: the *šopska salata* includes tomatoes, cucumber, onions and peppers topped with sheep milk cheese. *Kupus salata* is another delicacy: shredded cabbage with black olives in a light vinaigrette made with olive oil.

Those with a *sweet tooth* will have a hard time in Montenegro. There are no afternoon tea cakes and none of the classic pastries that are common in Western Europe. One solution can be found on the menu of the better restaurants: the *palačinke* (pancakes) the Austrians brought to Montenegro. The pancakes are filled with nuts or jam but there is a modern variety with Nutella *(eurokrem)*. With some luck, you might also find apple strudel *(štrudla od jabuka)* or plum cake *(pita od šljiva)* on the menu. Although many varieties of fruit grow in Montenegro, fruit salad *(voćna salata)* is rarely offered in restaurants. Ice cream *(sladoled)* is much more common. Tourists who risk the oriental *baklava* (puff pastry stuffed with nuts and raisins) should not overlook the glass of water served with it: it will help them swallow the sticky pastry. The various jams and marmalades that are sold at the markets and in the supermarkets are far too sweet for most tourists'

taste. However, *fig jam (marmelada od smokve)* is a really tasty speciality.

At any time of the day, you usually drink a typical *mocha* with your meal. It doesn't matter whether it's before or afterwards. If the strong coffee is

Goat's cheese and ham from Njeguši – *prijatno!*

too bitter for you, you can also ask for some milk. If you prefer, you can also drink your coffee with one of the typical *schnapps* or grappa. Plum brandy *šljivovica* is the favourite in the north, people on the coast prefer the Montenegrin grappa variety known as *loza* (with an alcoholic content of over 45 per cent). Now you're set: bon appétit *(prijatno)* and cheers *(živeli)*!

SHOPPING

A visit to a market in Montenegro is a very special shopping experience; most are held daily from the morning to the early afternoon. The farmers' markets in the cities are a real treat for the nose and the eyes: fragrant, colourful local produce lies spread out in all its splendour on wooden tables. The farmers' market in Bar on the Adriatic is especially worth a visit.

In addition, each Montenegrin village has its own market where all kinds of other goods are sold. Sometimes a farmers' market is also part of this and it is usually cheerful, loud and – above all – inexpensive. Every visitor to Montenegro should experience the spectacle at least once.

One of the most beautiful is the **INSIDER TIP** *market in Tuzi*, a small village between Podgorica and the Albanian border. A shopping spree here is a must if you are in the area. A wide choice of inexpensive clothing (but watch out for fake designer brands!) and hats made of fabric and leather as well as brooches with shells and wooden beer mugs are sold at the market. Of course, there are plenty of cheap products and tat on a market like this – but that's normal.

ARTS AND CRAFTS

The long winter evenings in the mountains in the north are the time for wood carving, knitting and crocheting. In former times, the mountain villages were snowed in from December to March and traditional handicrafts helped people pass the time and provided a lot of useful articles for the whole clan. Today, small families have also become more common in Montenegro but hand-crafted goods are still produced – for the tourists. The small works of art are sold directly in front of the house where large bowls decorated with floral motifs or simple boards and cutlery of all sizes await you. Wooden articles are offered at the markets and in the souvenir shops. But it is best to ignore those made of teak – they are cheap imports.

The ◉ wool pullovers might not be exactly haute couture but they are warm and cosy – and sometimes a bit scratchy. The reason is that the wool is not impregnated with any chemicals. Keep an eye out for hand-embroidered blouses and dresses or crocheted table cloths – they are still available, despite the cheap competition from imports.

Shopping Montenegrin style: the markets offer home-made products, fruit and vegetables grown locally, arts and crafts, and kitsch

FASHION

Fashion shops in Montenegro. There are elegant glass and marble boutiques selling exclusive brands such as Prada and Jil Sander and Italian shoes in chic Porto Montenegro. However, at the markets you can buy breezy cotton summer dresses for a mere 10 euros and local designer clothing is sold in the fashion boutiques in the old towns of Budva, Kotor, Herceg Novi and Podgorica. Long dresses with wide sleeves – many of the pieces have been inspired by traditional costumes and based on old patterns and quite a few are also decorated with ornaments made with silver or gold threads.

ICONS & MONASTERY PRODUCTS

You will not only be able to purchase icons, the pictures of Orthodox saints, at the various markets but also in the souvenir shops at the monasteries in the country. These icons do not cost very much and they are colourful and rather beautiful. And valuable or not: they have a special meaning for people. But you should not buy any expensive, "old" icons – they will almost certainly be fake.

In the monastery gift shops there is often home-produced honey or creams and lotions made by the nuns – all products are purely herbal.

SILVER JEWELLERY

Notably the Albanian silversmiths are popular for their filigree works. So look around for any number of quite inexpensive silver necklaces, rings and bracelets in Ulcinj, which is located directly on the Albanian border. Many of the jewellery shops are located on *Vlica zlatara* – even if the name is somewhat confusing: it means "street of the goldsmiths".

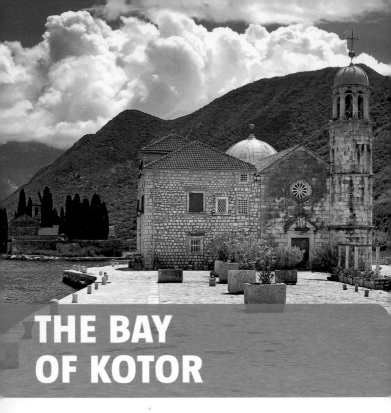

THE BAY OF KOTOR

No matter from where you approach it, the first view of the Bay of Kotor (Boka Kotorska), with its four inlets that cut deep into the mainland, will bowl you over.

Regardless of whether you catch the first glimpse shortly before landing at the airport in Tivat or after driving the scenic serpentine road down from Montenegro's own Olympus, the Lovćen, to Kotor: nowhere else in Montenegro do steep rock walls and the glittering green Adriatic meet as they do here. Of course, the natural scenery is unbeatable, but some amazing monuments were also created by man. From above, you can see the small church islands off the coast of Perast, Sv. Đorđe and Gospa od Škrpjela shine in the water like pebbles in a pool.

Stretching 28 km/17.4 mi into the hinterland, the Boka Kotorska – which the Montenegrins simply call Boka – offered seafarers a safe haven from the open waters of the Adriatic. The people living in the area, the *bokelji*, are extremely proud of a history of independence. Due to their sailing prowess, the Kotor fleet, under the flag of the Venetian Republic of San Marco, took part in combating the Turkish conquerors. Tsar Peter the Great took on the most famous seamen from the region to train his own captains.

Framed by the Orjen Mountains in the west and the Lovćen in the east, the Boka attracted ruling families and sailors from early times and the *bokelji* never really had any peace. When the Roman Empire split in AD 395, the bay became part of

Old ports and "pearls of nature": rugged mountains frame the heritage of proud seafarers in the only fjord in southern Europe

the Western Roman Empire while the rest of the Montenegrin coast was ceded to Byzantium. Its location at at the crossroads between east and west – between Constantinople and Venice, Vienna, Paris and and Moscow – meant that the foreign powers enriched the cosmopolitan spirit of the Boka through the centuries. The Venetians left the most significant traces in both the linguistic and culinary fields. Here, you will be served *cappuccino* and *risotto* more often than *ćevapčići* and *pite*.

The 70 km/43.5 mi coast road winds its way past palm trees, small beaches and charming old stone houses from Herceg Novi to Tivat – along with Kotor, the two largest cities on the bay. A ferry operates between Kamenari and Lepetane on the Verige Strait throughout the year making it possible to travel in no time from the old town of Kotor – with its unique ensemble – to Herceg Novi, the flower town.

The English poet George Gordon Byron visited the Bay of Kotor in 1809 and wrote: "At the birth of our planet, the most beautiful encounter between the land and the sea must have happened at the coast of Montenegro. When the pearls of nature were sown, handfuls of them were cast on this soil.' Beautifully poetic, Lord!

early February when thousands of people throng the waterfront promenade *(obala)* for the Mimosa Festival. The city's famous seafarers brought exotic plants with them when they returned from their

Visitors who have climbed Herceg Novis's 100,000 steps, relax in one of the cafés in the old town

HERCEG NOVI

MAP INSIDE BACK COVER
(126 C5) *(⚏ H5)* **The Yugoslavian Nobel Prize laureate Ivo Andrić described ★ Herceg Novi (pop. 14,000) as the city of "eternal greenery, sun and promenades".**

When the north of Montenegro is still in the grip of icy winter temperatures, the first flowers start to bloom in the harbour town that was founded in 1382 by the Bosnian King Tvrtko I and later named after Duke *(Herceg)* Stijepan Vukšić. This is celebrated every year with a feast of wine and fresh fish held in late January/

voyages and, paired with the flora of the Mediterranean region, they blossom in colourful splendour every spring. The mix of architectural styles from Oriental to Baroque lends Herceg Novi – wich is situated on a steep escarpment with long flights of steps – a touch of elegance that always charms its visitors.

The 7 km/4.4 mi long promenade *Šetalište Pet Danica* stretches from the spa town of Igalo to Meljine and is lined with cafés, restaurant and jetties. This is the place to see and be seen – with mirror sunglasses, the latest smartphones and chic designer clothes. The promenade forms the heart of the Herceg Nova Riviera that stretches from *Njivice* to *Ka-*

menari. The landmark mountain *Orjen* (1,893 m/6,211 ft) dominates the background, the sun rises over the Prevlaka Peninsula and sets behind the Mamula fortress island and there are especially beautiful views of all of this from the 🌊 promenade. Many holiday destinations on the beautiful Luštica Peninsula (see p. 47) are quickly accessed from Herceg Novi. There is also a ferry link.

The "City of 100,000 Steps" once again became the favourite holiday destination for Belgrade's artistic elite after the end of the Balkan wars. They are particularly attracted by the cultural activities offered in Herceg Novi (see pp. 108–109).

SIGHTSEEING

GALLERY JOSIP BEPO BENKOVIĆ ●
One of the oldest galleries in the country exhibits modern art by young talents from Serbia and Montenegro. New works are presented and awarded prizes at a winter salon in February, which has been organised by the collection since 1966.

May–Sept daily 9am–11pm, Oct–April 9am–5pm | Marka Vojnovića 4 | short. travel/mon7 | free admission

KANLI KULA
The fortress, which was constructed at the upper end of the old town during the Turkish period, served as a bastion and prison for many years. With seating for more than 1,000, Kanli Kula is now one of the most beautiful open air stages on the Adriatic. *Free admission on days without events*

STARI GRAD (OLD TOWN)
A flight of steps leads from *Nikole Đurković Square,* the city's bustling meeting place, with cafés and shops, in the centre of town, through Herceg Novi's most famous landmark the clock tower *(Sahat kula)* commissioned by Sultan Mahmud in 1667. The Orthodox Archangel Michael Church *(Sv. Arhanđela Mihaila)*, with its Romanesque, Gothic and Oriental elements, lies behind it on pretty, palm tree fringed *Herceg Stjepan Square*. The city's

---

⭐ **Herceg Novi**
Every year, the first place where spring can be felt in Montenegro is in the lovely flower town at the entrance to the Bay of Kotor → p. 34

⭐ **Stari grad (old town) in Kotor**
The architectural monuments behind Kotor's thick city walls recall centuries of fascinating history → p. 40

⭐ **Gospa od Škrpjela**
Built on top of shipwrecks and boulders, the Church of Our Lady of the Rocks, with its magnificent Baroque interior, perches in splendour off the coast of Perast → p. 42

⭐ **Perast**
The sleepy little town transports visitors back to a bygone era when illustrious captains put out to sea from here → p. 43

⭐ **Porto Montenegro**
Today, gigantic yachts bob up and down where warships used to lie at anchor: the harbour in Tivat has metamorphosed from a military base to a luxury marina → p. 45

⭐ **Luština**
Pristine bays, olive groves and deserted villages – the peninsula is a tranquil paradise → p. 47

MARCO POLO HIGHLIGHTS

archives take up the northern end of the square and there is a *library* with 30,000 volumes on the south side.

Follow the narrow streets down through the old town and you will land right in front of the entrance to the *Forte Marc*. The fortified tower was constructed between the 14th and 17th century and today films are shown here on a big screen in the summer.

TVRĐAVA ŠPANJOLA
(SPANISH FORTRESS) ⚓

Construction of this fortress, which towers over the city, was started by the Spaniards in 1538 and later completed by the Turks. Simply enjoy the magnificent views of the bay and Prevlaka Peninsula. *Free admission*

ZAVIČAJNI MUZEJ
(REGIONAL MUSEUM)

Archaeological finds from the early days of Herceg Novi – when Illyrians, Greeks and Romans settled in the area – are displayed on the two floors of the fine Museum. *Tue–Sun 8am–7.30pm | Mirka Komnenovića 9 | short.travel/mon8 | admission 3 euros*

FOOD & DRINK

Many pizzerias and restaurants serving grilled meat and fish line the *Šetalište Pet Danica*. And most of the city's beaches are turned into bars, pubs and discotheques in the evening. Find more information under *www.hercegnovi.travel*.

GRADSKA KAFANA –
RESTORAN TERASA DI PALMA

The gradska kafana, or town café, is the spot where locals like to spend their time for an espresso or generous meal. This café is also increasingly popular with tourists. The cuisine is international,

and the view from the ⚓ three terraces over the bay and old town is unforgettable. *Njegoševa 31 | tel. 031 32 40 67 | short.travel/mon10 | Moderate*

KONOBA KRUŠO

One of the best restaurants in town. It is so close to the sea the waves almost lap the entrance. Try *crni rižot*, black squid risotto. *Šetalište Pet Danica | tel. 031 32 32 38 | www.konobakruso.me | Moderate*

INSIDERTIP PETER'S PIE AND COFFEE ⚓

Don't say there's nothing healthy to eat in Montenegro! Here, you can order vegetarian, vegan and more. Served with good coffee and tea and a perfect promenade location with fabulous views. *Šetalište Pet Danica 18a | mobile 067 14 81 80 | Moderate*

SHOPPING

INSIDERTIP KNJIŽARA SO

The bookstore's name (So means "salt") is a reminder that Herceg Novi was established in the wake of the salt trade. It is located on the former "Salt Square" where the white gold was traded in times gone by. There is a wide selection of books in many languages and the staff members speak English. Browse your newly purchased books over a cup of coffee at one of the bars on the square. *Trg Nikole Đurkovića 3 | www.knjizaraso.com*

LEISURE & SPORTS

INSIDERTIP BARKARIOLI

The Italian word *barca* (boat) inspired the name of the local association of operators who offer boat excursions for tourists in Herceg Novi. The 25 boats ferry you for reasonable prices to the beaches

A holiday scene in Montenegro: the beach and sea in a historic setting – like in Herceg Novi

and towns in the Bay of Kotor. A barca is always available round-the-clock. *Topla 3 | at the harbour | mobile 067 30 09 43 | www.barkarioli.com*

GORBIS TRAVEL

The travel office not only organises private accommodation but also boat tours of the Bay of Kotor and day trips to Ostrog Monastery near Nikšić, as well as to Dubrovnik and Lake Skadar. *Njegoševa 66 | tel. 031 32 44 23 | www.gorbis.com*

TENISKI CENTAR SBS

In spring and autumn the site of two Grand Slam Tournaments. The court fees are 8 euros/hour; under floodlight, 12 euros. Lessons cost 15 euros/hour or 18 euros under floodlight. *Šetalište Pet Danica 8a | tel. 031 32 40 40*

BEACHES

The large hotels have manmade beaches (concrete platforms) and there is

INSIDER TIP a lovely sandy beach *(Blatna plaža)* at the western end of the promenade below the Igalo Institute. Those who prefer to swim further away from town should take the small coastal road towards Bijela where the beaches in *Zelenika, Kumbor, Đenovići* and *Balošići* are not as crowded as those in Herceg Novi. Boats leave the harbour for *Njivice*, where the nudist beach of the Hotel Riviera is also open to non-guests. The beautiful beaches on the *Luštica Peninsula* can also be easily reached by boat in 10 minutes. One thing applies here and for all the other beaches in the Bay of Kotor: as there is hardly any inflow from the sea, the water sometimes becomes a little stagnant.

ENTERTAINMENT

The promenade along the shore stretches for about a mile and is lined with countless bars, cafés, pubs and restaurants. On balmy summer evenings the locals meet up by the sea. Party goes on here until the early hours of the morning: in the *Bolivar* (local bands), *Casa* (house and techno), *Nautica* (jazz), and *Copas* (with sun loungers on the beach itself).

WHERE TO STAY

Herceg Novi is one of the more expensive locations but there are also some more

where film classics are shown in the original version. *10 rooms | Šetalište Pet Danica 42 | mobile 067 55 23 19 | aurora hotel.me | Moderate*

GUEST HOUSE GOJKOVIC ☆

Three double rooms with a shared bathroom doesn't sound that glamourous at first – but every room has a balcony and sea view. The family (the son speaks

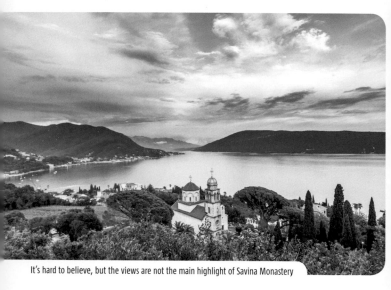

It's hard to believe, but the views are not the main highlight of Savina Monastery

economical hotels, holiday apartments and private accommodation in the city that cost between 10 and 20 euros. There is still a great deal of construction activity taking place and it can be noisy in off-season.

INSIDER TIP ▶ AURORA

The director Emir Kusturica ("Underground", "Arizona Dream") bought the venerable Hotel Aurora on the promenade along the shore and tastefully developed it. The boutique hotel has an excellent ● cinema on the ground floor

fluent English) greets you with a warm welcome. And the prices are exceptionally reasonable! *3 rooms | Dr Jovana Bijelića 19/18 | booking at www.booking. com | Budget*

PERLA

Here, you can stay overnight by the seaside on the promenade of Herceg Novi. The rooms are pleasant, the terrace is even lovelier and the breakfast- and dinner buffet are first-class. *41 rooms | Šetalište Pet Danica 98 | tel. 031 34 57 00 | www.perla.me | Budget–Moderate*

Jova Dabovića 12 | tel. 031 35 08 20 | www.hercegnovi.travel

WHERE TO GO

BIJELA ● (127 D5) (*⚘ J5*)

The community (pop. 4,000) 14 km/8.7 mi from Herceg Novi is the ideal place for divers and other water sports enthusiasts to spend their Boka holiday. The *Hotel Delfin (112 rooms | tel. 031 68 34 00 | www.hoteldelfin.me | Moderate–Expensive)* has facilities for weight lifting, boxing, judo and tennis, football and basketball. The *Regional Center for Divers Training (tel. 031 68 34 77 | www.rcud.me)* organises courses for beginners and advanced divers. The *Villa Azzurro (tel. 031 67 16 06 | Moderate–Expensive)*, with 14 rooms, at the south end of Bijela welcomes its guests to its own beach. In *Morinj*, 8 km/5 mi towards Kotor, you can dine elegantly in the atmospheric old mill INSIDER TIP *Čatovića Mlini (tel. 032 37 30 30 | www.catovica-mlini.com | Moderate–Expensive)*. It has been considered one of the best restaurants in the country for many years and serves excellent fish. Reservations are essential in the season.

IGALO (126 C5) (*⚘ H5*)

The spa town (pop. 3,000) is situated at the west end of the promenade, only a 15-minute walk from the harbour of Herceg Novi. Rheumatics have long appreciated the beneficial effects of the minerals in the mud from the shallow sea, and the first health centre was built here in 1950. Today, the spa and wellness facilities at the ● *Institut Igalo* or *Mediterranean Health Center (420 rooms | Save Ilica 1 | tel. 031 65 85 55 | www.igalospa.com | Moderate)* match Western European standards, though at more reasonable prices. Lower-priced accommodation than at the Institut is available in many private rooms and small hotels *(info at www.hercegnovi.travel)*. There are several camping sites along the coast. Adjacent to the Institut Igalo you can visit the Villa Galeb *(admission 3 euros)*. The majestic luxury villa was commissioned as a summer residence by the former Yugoslavian president Tito during the 1960s.

SAVINA (126 C5) (*⚘ H5*)

The small village (pop. 1,000) set in lush greenery is only a twenty-minute walk away from the harbour in Herceg Novi. The Orthodox monastery (daily 7am–7pm) with its two churches a little bit above the waterfront promenade has the almost 800-year-old INSIDER TIP Bishop's Cross of Saint Sava, the patron saint of the Serbian Orthodox church, in its treasury.

KOTOR

🏛 MAP ON P. 127

(127 E–F 4–5) (*⚘ K5*) **Wake up in the morning to the sound of bells chiming – there are almost a dozen churches in the historic old part of Kotor (pop. 6,000). The area was declared a Unesco World Heritage Site after the earthquake in the year 1979 to ensure that it was reconstructed without delay.** Every day, the people living in Kotor realise that this has been successful when they relax in one of the cafés on the square – polished smooth by countless footsteps – in front of the clock tower. This is probably the best place to get a feeling for the spirit of the city. A visit to Kotor means immersing oneself in the Middle Ages when the small town at the south-east corner of the bay was dominated by the Venetians. Kotor is home

to the Cathedral of Saint Tryphon built on the foundations of a 9th century church in 1166. Kotor's ancient walls reflect the self-assurance of the independent seafarers' community that always withstood the on-slaught of the Turks. It was once named Dekadron and then Catarum, Catera and Cathara by a changing series of rulers. The name of Kotor prevailed among the South Slavs. Today, that is even more appropriate: *Kot* means "cat" in Monte-negrin – and the town is full of them!

There is a row of picturesque villages along the coast towards Herceg Novi that all have magnificent views of the bay and that are within easy reach by public bus. Plenty of cruise- and excursion boats navigate the tight estuary; unfortunately, along with the many day-trippers they bring more pollution as well!

SIGHTSEEING

INSIDER TIP JEWISH CEMETERY
The Jews who came to Montenegro from the Iberian Peninsula in the Middle Ages were known as "Spanish Jews". The country's new Jewish community – newly founded only in 2011 – has not been able to find any written documents on Jewish life in the country in mediaeval times. But the cemetery in Kotor provides sufficient proof that Jews have lived here for centu-ries. It is in fact the only Jewish cemetery in Montenegro and one of the few in the Balkans. In the district of Škaljari

POMORSKI MUZEJ (MARITIME MUSEUM) ●
The three floors of the former palace of the Grgurina family houses an exhibi-tion of sailor's clothing, models of old ships, typical weapons and a relief map of the bay. *15 April–June, Sept–Oct Mon–Sat 8am–6pm, Sun 9am–1pm, July–Aug Mon–Sat 8am–8pm, Sun 10am–4pm,*

Nov–14 April Mon–Fri 8am–3pm, Sat/Sun 9am–1pm | Trg Bokeljske mornarice | www.museummaritimum.com | admis-sion 4 euros

CITY WALLS
Begun in 1420 by the Venetians the 4 km/2.5 mi long city walls, which cut deeply into the mountain above Kotor, were not completed until 400 years later. The ascent begins just after the northern gate, and there is another entrance be-hind the clock tower. On the way to the fortress 🔅 *Sv. Ivan (free admission)* you have to pace yourself: there are 1,350 stone steps to climb. You also have to give way to people making their descent. But the panoramic views on the way and at the top are magnificent! That makes up for everything. *Admission 8 euros*

STARI GRAD (OLD TOWN) ★ ●
Three gates lead into the historic old town of Kotor; the oldest is the one in the south that was built as early as the 13th century. The northern and main gate *(Morska vrata)* in front of the large car park on the shore – the old town is a pedestrian zone – were built in the Re-naissance style in the 16th century. The *clock tower (Sat kula)* is opposite the main gate with the palaces of the patri-cian Bisanti and Beskuca families in the background. In addition to the *Saint Luka Church*, which was shared by Catholic and Orthodox worshipers until well into the 19th century, the *Saint Tryphon Cathedral* is especially worth visiting. It suffered se-vere damage in the 1979 earthquake but has since been completely restored.

FOOD & DRINK

BASTION
The restaurant at the northern entrance to the old town offers a splendid range of

fresh fish. Try the **INSIDER TIP** squid stuffed with ham and cheese. *Trg od drva | tel. 032 32 21 16 | www.bastion123.com | Moderate*

GALION ⌇

Enjoy the exquisite cuisine of this restaurant right on the waterfront overlooking the old town, and choose between 130 imported and local wines. *Šurani | tel. 032 32 50 54 | Moderate–Expensive*

Square) and it has all of the trimmings you would expect to find in a trendy disco. On the other hand, if you prefer things more peaceful, the *Old Winery Bar (Zanatsla 483)* in the old town is perfect.

WHERE TO STAY

HOSTEL OLD TOWN

The building dates from the 13th century and in some rooms the original walls

This is where you feel the spirit of this old town: the square in front of the clock tower in Kotor

KONOBA CESARICA

A successful combination: excellent seafood, delicious fish and meat dishes, friendly service and very moderate prices plus a charming atmosphere. *Stari grad 375 | tel. 032 33 60 93 | Moderate*

ENTERTAINMENT

The *Diskoteka Maximus (discomaximus. me)* is located on *Trg oružja* (Weapon

are left exposed. As a guest you can hire bicycles from the hostel. *5 rooms, 1 apartment., 12 5- to 12-bed dormitories | Stari grad 284 | tel. 032 32 53 17 | www.hostel-kotor.me | Budget*

MARIJA

An old townhouse in a fantastic location in the heart of the old town. That's why it tends to be quite loud in the evenings and at night, and finding a parking space can also be tricky. *17 rooms | Stari grad*

449 | tel. 032 32 50 62 | www.hotelmarija. me | Budget

HOTEL MONTE CRISTO
Don't miss out on this authentic Kotor experience: situated in the old town, spacious and comfortable rooms and some with the old stone walls. The staff are also incredibly pleasant and friendly. Not cheap, but affordable. *5 rooms | Stari grad | booking at www.booking.com | Moderate–Expensive*

VARDAR
An old patrician house with 33 rooms, Turkish bath and cigar lounge in the old part of town, surrounded by stone houses. Ask for ✹ INSIDER TIP room 206 as Kotor's elegant promenade is right below its balcony. *Trg od drva | tel. 032 32 50 84 | www.hotelvardar.com | Expensive*

LOW BUDGET

The small but elegant family-run guest house Arnaut *(14 rooms | Njegoševa 111 | mobile 069 63 23 53 | www.pansionarnaut.net)* is in the centre of Herceg Novi and inexpensive for this town. Even in August, a double room costs less than 20 euros, and drops to approx. 10 euros in the off season. Prices are negotiable from October to May.

You cannot go wrong at the snack bar Buregdzinica "AS" *(Palih Boraca | mobile 069 50 52 13)* in Tivat. The Turkish borek tastes excellent and there is even freshly squeezed juice. Super friendly and amazingly low prices!

INFORMATION
Stari grad 315 | tel. 032 32 59 50 | www. tokotor.me

WHERE TO GO

DOBROTA (127 E4) (⊞ K4–5)
This suburb of Kotor (pop. 7,000) has many small beaches and stretches for more than 7 km/4.4 mi along the coast. The *Ellas Restaurant (mobile 069 22 04 55 | www.restoranelas.com | Budget–Moderate)* on the waterfront offers something a little different as it specialises in Greek food. There are simple multi-bed rooms in the *Dobrotski Dvori guesthouse (8 rooms | tel. 032 33 08 40 | Budget)*, also on the coast. If you want to spend the night in more elegant surroundings then you should book into the *Palazzo Radomiri (tel. 032 33 31 72 | www.palazzoradomiri.com | Expensive)*. A Russian Montenegrin family has renovated the 18th century Baroque palace and each of the seven rooms has been named after the ships that once belonged to the Radomiri family. Although it is directly on the waterfront, it also has a swimming pool.

GOSPA OD ŠKRPJELA ★
(127 D4) (⊞ J4)
One of the highlights of any Boka trip is a visit to the two church islands off the coast near Perast. The original Gospa od Škrpjela (Our Lady of the Rocks) was built in 1452. Every year, boats sail across on 22 July to celebrate the anniversary by throwing stones into the water around the island. This custom has a long tradition: for decades, sailors and fishermen sunk boats and piled up boulders on what was originally the small area of the rock until, in the middle of the 17th century, there was enough space to expand

The magnificently decorated interior of the Gospa od Škrpjela

the church and add some new buildings. The house of worship was given its Baroque interior by the architect Ilija Katičić who added the bell tower and improved the nave of the church. The hundreds of votive pictures in the church showing ships and scenes of everyday life in Perast are tokens of appreciation for being healed of a disease.

The island *Sv. Đorđe* (Saint George), opposite Gospa od Škrpjela, was for a long period the most important Benedictine abbey in the bay. In contrast to its sister church, Sv. Đorđe dominates the scene from atop a natural stone reef. Boat tours can be booked in all of the towns and villages on the coast.

PERAST ⭐ (127 D–E4) (🛍 J4)

Perast, about 14 km/8.7 mi from Kotor, is considered one of the most beautiful Baroque towns on the Adriatic and is a protected heritage site. The busts in front of the 15th century Baroque *St Nikola church*, with its 55 m/180.4 ft high bell tower, indicate what the village is famous for: its captains, who also taught Tsar Peter the Great's sailors all they knew. Today, only around 300 people live in Perast but, at one time, the fleet of this community (that was declared autonomous in 1558) was larger than that of Dubrovnik.

Under Venetian rule for centuries, it was repeatedly attacked by the ships of the Ottoman Empire but they were never able to take the city. Its status as an important border town gave its inhabitants many privileges that ended abruptly with the fall of Venice in 1797 and led to the downfall of the proud fraternity of seamen. The Museum *(April–Oct daily 9am–9pm, Nov–March daily 9am–3pm | on the shore | www.muzejperast. me | admission 4.50 euros)* of Perast is located in the Bujović Palace from the

Always worth a visit, even if you're not a yacht owner: Porto Montenegro

17th century. Portraits of the city's illustrious captains, maps and the furnishings of the Bujović's make it possible for visitors to immerse themselves in the bygone world of the seafarers. The ☼ INSIDER TIP *Hotel Conte (10 apartments | Obala Kapetana Marka Martinovića | tel. 032 37 36 87 | www.hotelconte.me | Expensive)* will overwhelm you with its great apartments and spectacular views. The restaurant is right on the sea and you simply must try the grilled scampi.

PRČANJ (127 E4) (*ロ K4*)
Prčanj (pop. 1,000) is around 6 km/ 3.7 mi from Kotor on the bay. The town's seamen established the first postal service between Venice and Constantinople in the 17th century. There is a monument to Prčanj's most famous captain, Ivo Visin, in front of the parish church *Bogordični hram*, the largest in the Boka. The hotel INSIDER TIP *Splendido (43 rooms | Naselje Glavati | tel. 032 30 17 00 | www.splendido-hotel.com | Expensive)*, with swimming pool and direct access to the sea, is named after the ship Visin used for his circumnavigation of the world. The *Art Hotel Galathea (7 rooms | Jadranska magistrala 134 | tel. 032 33 74 31 | www.septemberhotels. com | Expensive)* is in a century-old stone building and you are only 10 m/32.8 ft away from the on-site beach.

RISAN (127 D3–4) (*ロ J4*)
The Illyrian Queen Teuta established her residence in the oldest town on the bay (pop. 1,500), which is around 18 km/11.2 mi from Kotor, in the 3rd century BC before being driven off by the Romans about 100 years later. The mosaic floors from the Roman period, when Risan was the most important town in the region, can be seen in an *open air museum (always open | admission 3.50 euros)* a short way above the filling station.

TIVAT

(127 E5) *(∭ J5)* **Once a sleepy place, it has been blessed with luxury. Tivat (pop. 9,400) is renowned for the superyachts berthed in its harbour.**

The city was controlled by the Venetians until 1797, followed by the Austro-Hungarian Empire that took advantage of Tivat's strategic location at the entrance to the bay to develop a naval base. Warships were still anchored in Tivat in the 20th century: the town was the most important military base in the southern Adriatic in Tito's era. It was barred for tourism for a long time, and the city with its nearby airport was only gradually opened during the second half of the 20th century. However, it remained more a transit hub than holiday destination. In 2006, the Canadian billionaire Peter Munk bought the run-down shipyards and promised to build Europe's best marina. No sooner said than done: ★ *Porto Montenegro (www.portomontenegro. com)* is about to claim the top spot from Monte Carlo. Vast luxury yachts have their port home here. The Mediterranean Yacht Brokers Association displays the dream vessels in September at the *MYBA Pop-up Superyacht Show (www. mybapopupshow.com)*. Directly by the waterside the town has expanded with noble apartments – 10 ft^2 cost up to 10,000 euros. The luxury hotel *Regent Porto Montenegro (86 rooms | tel. 032 66 06 60 | www.regenthotels.com/porto montenegro | Expensive)* also has steep prices, although there are no complaints about a lack of clientele.

SIGHTSEEING

YUGOSLAVIAN GENERAL CONSULATE
Pardon? Yugoslavia is already ancient history! The former state still has a general consulate in Tivat. The telephone number is identical to the founding date of the Socialist republic (29.11.43). Devotional objects such as flags and old postcards are on display in droves. And you can be issued with a "genuine" Yugoslavian passport for a mere 10 euros. *Daily 10am–5pm | Palih Borača 4 | free admission*

MUSEUM ARSENAL
Take a risk and tour an original submarine, complete with that claustrophobic feeling. In front of the former navy yard is the showpiece of the Yugoslavian navy called INSIDER TIP *Heroj*, "Hero". There is not much to see inside the museum. But it is worth a visit to see the submarine. *Mon–Fri 9am–6pm, Sat 1pm–5pm | admissions museum 3 euros, submarine plus 2 euros*

FOOD & DRINK

BIG BEN
If you love pizza – and who doesn't? – then don't miss this friendly restaurant. The fish, meat, coffee and cake are also excellent, and there is a fabulous view from the ☼ terrace. *Šetalište Seljanovo 21 | tel. 067 37 14 66 | Moderate*

INSIDER TIP BYBLOS ☼
Lamps like Aladdin's, old-fashioned seating corners, oriental flair – the Lebanese restaurant is something special. Enjoy the delicious starters (meza), lamb with fresh mint and yogurt or pomegranate sauce and the view of the luxury yachts in the harbour. *Mobile 063 22 20 23 | www.byblos.me | Moderate–Expensive)*

KONOBA BACCHUS
The restaurant is a little out of the way and very reasonable. Obviously, plenty of locals come here. Excellent fish dishes.

The squid filled with crab is especially delicious! *Palih Borača | tel. 032 67 25 58 | Moderate*

ONE
An attractive place to sip a pro secco and enjoy a meal on the main promenade of Porto Montenegro. Has also very good breakfast. *Mobile 067 48 60 45 | www.facebook.com/jettyone | Moderate–Expensive*

SHOPPING

In the labyrinthine streets of Porto Montenegro luxury boutiques such as Gaultier or Stella McCartney offer a glimpse of the world of the rich and beautiful. Here, you will learn the meaning of the Montenegrins' word for window shopping – pariti oči – or "watery eyes". On four dates during the summer the streets of Porto Montenegro host the ● *farmer's market*. Wine and dine on organic produce is the motto: you can sample and buy honey, cheese, olive oil and ham from the mountain regions. The dates are advertised on *www.portomontenegro.com*.

LEISURE & SPORTS

Porto Montenegro offers a wide range of luxury wellness centres. In the ● ☼ *Yacht Club Pool (short.travel/ mon15)* you have to pay 42 euros as a non-resident, but you can splash around in a large pool with fantastic views and enjoy the music and club atmosphere. The spa *Pura Vida (www.puravida-spa.com)* offers a chocolate treatment, 90 minutes cost 120 euros. A full body massage is offered from 30 euros for 30 minutes.

BEACHES

In the nearby town of Oblatno, *Almara Beach (www.almara.me)* offers sheer luxury. In addition to the standard sun loungers and sun canopies you can rent a "living room" – for a mere 500 euros a day. This includes relaxation under a white canopy with sofas, chairs and plasma TV as well as a butler and cocktails. Not enough cash with you? The public beaches in Tivat and nearby villages offer similar relaxation. Two sun loungers and a canopy cost 5 to 10 euros here. *Gradska* is located in Tivat near the Hotel Palma.

WHERE TO STAY

PALMA ☼
Formerly a grey state-run hotel, now the building has been recently refurbished. A high standard, with a splendid view of the bay and private beach. *114 rooms | Pakovo | tel. 032 67 22 88 | Moderate*

PINE
Modern rooms and a unique location on the pedestrian promenade and a really delicious breakfast buffet. *26 rooms | tel. 032 67 13 05 | htpmimoza.me | Moderate*

ROOMS TAMARA
Why always stay in a hotel? These apartments (some with balconies) are very spacious, pleasant and very reasonable. A private pool 400 m/1,312 ft to the beach. *5 apartments. | Župa bb | mobile 068 51 49 36 | booking at www.booking. com | Budget*

VILLA ROYAL
The attractive new building is located behind the marina. *6 rooms, 6 apartments | Kalimanj | tel. 032 67 53 10 | Moderate*

INFORMATION
Palih Borača 19 | tel. 032 67 13 23 | www. tivat.travel

WHERE TO GO

LUŠTICA ★ ●
(126–127 C–E 5–6) (𝄽 H–J 5–6)

The Montenegrins call this 18 mi² peninsula just south of Tivat the "Land of Olives". Olive trees have grown here since ancient times and most of the houses used to have their own mills; the people here lived with – and from – olives. Later Luštica came under the control of the military that guarded the entrance to the Bay of Kotor from here. Many residents departed and left behind abandoned villages. Now their grandchildren are returning to Luštica and with them foreign investors. Luxury resorts, marinas and golf courses are springing up everywhere. The 35 km/21.8 mi long coastline is still fairly empty and the unspoiled bays with their turquoise water lie secluded in the sun, the beaches of *Žanjice, Mirište, Dobreč* and *Arza* are particularly beautiful. The interior of Luštica is also charming: deserted villages, stone houses in the shade of olive groves, and all of that in clear, fresh air; *Obosnik* Mountain is 582 m/1,909 ft high. The olive trees are also growing again (see p. 19).

On the western side of the peninsula is INSIDERTIP *Rose*, "Montenegro's Saint-Tropez". Serbian film stars have settled here – and you'll feel like a star when you stroll elegantly through the chic village: roses and oleanders cover the walls of the magnificently renovated stone houses, palm trees provide shade and the beach is on the doorstep. And Herceg Novi, which you can see from the bedroom windows with a bit of luck, is accessible by boat within a few minutes. Tourists can now also rent apartments in Rose; just a few metres away from the sea are the 15 bungalows – for two to four persons – of the *Forte Rose (mobile*

Welcome to Luštica Peninsula, the "Land of the Olives"!

067 37 73 11 | www.forterose.me | Moderate). Modra Špilja, the Blue Grotto, is on the south side of Luštica and can only be reached by sea. Boat tours leave from Tivat (information at the tourist office, see "Information" above) and *Herceg Novi (Barkarioli | mobile 067 55 53 36).*

THE ADRIATIC

Beaches stretching for miles and picturesque bays, small sections of sandy coast hidden between the rocks and a green hinterland that almost reaches the shore. This is Montenegro's Adriatic coast.

The peaks of the Lovćen and Rumija soar up into the sky behind the delightful little harbour towns on the coast and offer everyone who is travelling over the mountains from Podgorica or Cetinje majestic views from the heights. A picturesque landscape stretches from Budva to the island of Ada Bojana just before the Albanian border: small fishing boats rocked gently by the waves, countless olive groves hidden in the beautiful hills, stone houses from another era and avenues lined with pine trees and cypresses – you already get that holiday feeling before you've even arrived at the beach. The Montenegrin Adriatic remained undiscovered as a tourist destination for many years. There were only two hotels in Budva before the Second World War. In the 1960s construction was begun on the coast road – the Jadranska magistrala, that runs from Bar to Rijeka in northern Croatia – and ushered in a new era. Hotels sprung up in next to no time. Flocks of tourists – mainly from Germany, Austria and Switzerland – flowed into the country. All of a sudden, German was spoken in Montenegro – the waiters and maids took crash courses to learn a smattering of the language.

Ulcinj near the border to Albania, which seemed to be at the end of the world, became a destination for tourists from

Photo: Beach near Petrovac na Moru

Magnificent scenery on the Montenegrin Riviera: long beaches and picturesque towns surrounded by green hills

the German Democratic Republic. They spent their holidays there in large groups, watched over and strictly segregated from holidaymakers from West Germany. One highlight of the trip was a coach excursion to Dubrovnik – not all East Germans made it back to their hotel; many took the opportunity to escape to the West.

The second wave of construction began after the 1979 earthquake. The people living on the coast in particular were given favourable loans to renovate and make alterations to the houses. The first *vikendice*, weekend cottages, were built. Today, the Montenegrin Adriatic is a real gem in spite of the congested roads. Foreign conquerors left enchanting architectural traces in Budva, Stari Bar and the old town in Ulcinj –Illyrians, Romans, Venetians and Austrians occupied and defended the harbour towns for centuries. The border between the Byzantine and Roman Empires ran south of Budva. The Sozina Tunnel *(2.50 euros)* has shortened the travel time from the

In the ruins of Stari Bar you can take a stroll back almost 1,000 years in time

interior of the country to the coast near Sutomore by many miles and scores of visitors from Podgorica use it in summer. However, in the middle of the tunnel the police like to set up speed checks and it seems to be very lucrative. But you will find the winding ● road from Virpazar near Petrovac more interesting. It runs through a unique area: on one side a lunar landscape and on the other breathtaking views of the Adriatic coast. Better still, you will also save on the tunnel toll!

BAR

(130 A–B 4–5) *(🗺 P7)* **The city has developed rapidly in the past decades. Bar (pop. 13,500) now has a network of wide streets and boulevards. Construction is everywhere and there are high-rise buildings and shopping malls shooting up all over.**

Bar's population is young – courses at the faculties of journalism and business administration are sought after by students from all parts of Montenegro. The city is also increasingly becoming the cultural and economic centre of the southern Adriatic. The marina has moorings for 900 vessels, the harbour is abuzz with activity. The permanent ferry connections to Bari, as well as the railroad from Belgrade, bring many tourists into the city. Although most are headed to one of the nearby vacation spots, Bar still profits from them.

SIGHTSEEING

GRADSKI MUZEJ (CITY MUSEUM)
Artefacts from many centuries are on display in the former summer residence of King Nikola I on the waterfront promenade. *Daily 8am–10pm | Šetalište Kralja Nikole | admission 1.50 euro*

FOOD & DRINK

Even if the town's classic attractions are few and far between, you will not regret your visit: at the ☼ promenade in the harbour of Bar you can enjoy a meal with views of the sailing yachts.

KNJAŽEVA BAŠTA
Fine dining in the garden of the former royal residence. Since no king lives here, instead you can enjoy the princely service. *Šetalište Kralja Nikole | mobile 069 09 04 99 | www.knjazevabasta.com | Moderate*

SAVOIA
Just around the corner from the farmer's market. From pizza to seafood, everything is reasonably priced. The grilled squid is delicious. The desserts and coffee are also excellent and the same goes for the Montenegrin wines. *Jovana Tomaševića 16 | mobile 069 63 33 33 | Budget –Moderate*

SHOPPING

Large supermarkets are located in the centre of Bar. But on no account should you miss the INSIDER TIP *farmers' market (7am–2pm | Bar pijaca)*, which is also held in the city centre. Vast quantities of fruit and vegetables, fresh fish, heavy hams, honey and olive oil, bay leaves and rosemary, every possible kind of goat's cheese – a colourful selection of all the region's produce – are sold here and the aroma is heavenly!

WHERE TO STAY

Most tourists only come here to browse and shop, as it is more pleasant to stay in Sutomore (see p. 60) or Šušanj. Both bays are near the town and are accessible on foot or by bicycle.

Of course, in Bar there are now several attractive and reasonable apartments. A great example is the *Apartment Ines (Železnička stanica | booking at www.booking.com)* where you only pay 35 euros for up to 600 ft² for four people and what's more, the owners are super friendly.

★ **Stari Bar**
Visit to the past: the ruins of Stari Bar lie at the foot of Mount Rumija → **p. 52**

★ **Stari grad (old town) in Budva**
The centuries-old heritage of the Venetians stands proudly between stone walls on a small peninsula → **p. 53**

★ **Sv. Stefan**
The most beautiful photo opportunity in the country and a meeting place for the rich, the famous and the beautiful: what was once a fishermen's island has been transformed into a luxurious hotel → **p. 56**

★ **Petrovac na Moru**
Old houses on the promenade and palm trees on the beach: the small coastal village has managed to retain much of its charm → **p. 57**

★ **Buljarica**
Unimpaired views of the beach and sea from where the ground is too wet to support development → **p. 59**

★ **Velika plaža (Grand Beach) in Ulcinj**
The longest beach in Montenegro is very popular with both children and surfers: the former love the shallow water; the latter, the strong winds → **p. 62**

MARCO POLO HIGHLIGHTS

Obala 13. Jula | tel. 030 3116 33 | www.visitbar.org

DOBRA VODA AND UTJEHA
(130 C4–5) (*ш P–Q 7–8*)

The 10–15 km/6.2–9.3 mi drive to the nearby bays is worth it: there are very inexpensive holiday apartments and rooms, the sea is on the doorstep, cy-

presidentutjeha.com | Budget) are set in an olive grove. The restaurant *(Moderate–Expensive)* serves grilled dishes.

OLIVE TREES (130 B4) (*ш P7*)

Between Bar and Ulcinj there are about 175,000 olive trees, many of them have been here for 2,000 years. The oldest tree – also one of the oldest trees worldwide – is reputed to be 2,200 years old. It is about 5 km/3.1 mi away from Bar near the village of Tomba on the old road from Stari Bar to Ulcinj.

Display window to the time of Venetic rule: the old town of Budva

presses and pine trees surround the area and the chirping of the crickets is thrown in for free. It is the most lovely in May when the ● broom is in full blossom and the region is a sea of yellow. *Ani Apartmani (mobile 069 02 76 86 | www.ani-apartmani.com | Budget)* rents 14 large, modern holiday apartments in Dobra Voda. Some of the bungalows in President Utjeha *(8 apartments, 4 bungalows | mobile 068 45 64 85 | www.*

STARI BAR ★ (130 B4) (*ш P7*)

New life has been breathed into the small town that was long deserted. Old *(stari)*, historic Bar is located about 4 km/2.5 mi north of Bar and 18 km/11.2 mi from Ulcinj at the ascent to Mount Rumija. The origins of the city, which is surrounded by a mighty wall, can be traced back to the 11th century when Bar was part of the Serbian coastal state of Zeta. The *city gate*, whose façade was reconstructed in the 14th century, also dates from this period. *St George's Cathedral* was erected in the Romanesque Gothic style in the 12th century. The remains of an even older church have been discovered beneath its walls. There are also traces of the time the Turks occupied the city; one of the buildings from this period is the old *hammam*. *June–Oct open all day | admission 1 euro.* On the main street is the traditional ● **INSIDER TIP** *patisserie Karađuzović (mobile 069 03 18 62)*, where you not only enjoy a good mocha coffee but also one of the region's best Baklava. If you're going to be naughty, why not here?

BUDVA

MAP INSIDE BACK COVER
(128 C5–6) (⌀ L–M6) **The oldest city on the Montenegrin coast (pop. 13,300) is already clearly visible from a distance – no matter whether you drive down from Cetinje or arrive from Tivat.**

The historic heart of the city lies on a peninsula in the Adriatic a short distance away from the rest of the coast and stretches towards the island of *Sv. Nikola*. The Venetians gave the old town its magnificent appearance in the 15th century; Budva was only slightly damaged in the earthquake in 1979 and any traces of this have long disappeared.

No community in Montenegro has grown as quickly as Budva. The sell-out of property started immediately after the Balkan wars and today even the neighbouring mountains have been built on and integrated into the city. Living in the mountains with a pool and sea view is now all the rage because the city is often overcrowded – especially in summer. There is an acute lack of parking space, the roads around the town are jammed and water is short in the high season. But Budva has still remained a magnet for visitors that particularly draws in Serbs and Russians: the city with the most beautiful girls, the flashiest cars and highest prices on the coast also boasts the longest nights in the discos, good food on the waterfront promenade and designer shops in the old town.

SIGHTSEEING

CITADELA (CITADEL)
The old fortress in front of the main square in the old section of town becomes an open air theatre in summer. A few models of old ships – including one of Columbus' "Santa Maria" – are on display inside. ● *Free admission*

MUZEJ GRADA BUDVE (CITY MUSEUM)
The museum, possibly the most beautiful in the country, presents you Budva's long history dating back to the 5th century BC. Clay bowls and jugs, metal tools and coins from the Roman period are displayed to illustrate the past of what was once an Illyrian settlement. *Daily 9am–midnight | Petrovića 11 | admission 2 euros*

STARI GRAD (OLD TOWN) ★
All that's missing is St Mark's Square and the Canal Grande: although the city's rulers changed frequently, the Venetians left the strongest legacy after they had conquered Budva in 1442. In particular, they built many churches as well as the still well-preserved city wall. The 9th century triple-nave *Church of Saint John the Baptist (Sv. Ivan)* and the *bell tower (Sahat kula)*, which was erected in 1867, are also worth seeing.

BUDVA

FOOD & DRINK

In Budva, food is usually more expensive than in other coastal villages, but the cuisine is fine quality. There are some more reasonably priced restaurants – check the prices at the entrance.

JADRAN – KOD KRSTA
If you like seafood, you will love this restaurant right at the harbour. The menu lists fresh fish and typical Montenegrin meat dishes as well as INSIDER TIP reasonably priced set meals of the day. *Slovenska obala 10 | tel. 033 45 10 28 | www.restaurantjadran.com | Moderate– Expensive*

KONOBA PORTUN
Small, quiet, authentic and in the old town. Polite service, the friendly owners have plenty of good tips. The squid is delicious. *Stjepana Mitrova Ljubiše 5 | mobile 068 41 25 36 | Moderate*

RESTORAN PORTO
Dine in a romantic location at the gates of the old town in the yachting harbour. Fish and scampi swim in a small tank and are freshly prepared. *Marina Budva | tel. 033 45 15 98 | www.restoranporto.com | Moderate–Expensive*

VERDE
Sometimes, a restaurant like this is just right: not too many frills, fast service, extremely reasonable, simple but good. And something for vegetarians as well. The menu is in English. *Velji Vinogradi | mobile 063 21 44 06 | Budget*

LEISURE & SPORTS

Budva's beaches like Jaz or Slovenska plaža are a true paradise for fitness fanatics and sports fans. There is a wide range of sports from bungee jumping, jet skiing to surfing, snorkelling and diving. You can book fish picnics and boat excursions along the coast in many of the local tourist offices.

BEACHES

JAZ
The almost endlessly long pebble beach at Jaz is only around 5 km/3.1 mi from Budva towards Tivat. The rock concerts held at Jaz are legendary: the Rolling Stones and Madonna have both performed here!

MOGREN I AND II
Here, things are a little more peaceful than at the town beach Jaz and Slovenska plaža. And it's only a few minutes away from Hotel Avala. A handful of cafés and pubs serve refreshments and it is also possible to hire pedal boats.

SLOVENSKA PLAŽA
The long shingle beach stretches for a few hundred feet from the harbour to the end of the bay at Budva in the direction of Bečići and offers a wide range of restaurants apart from many sporting opportunities.

ENTERTAINMENT

Budva is one large nightclub. The Montenegrins love loud music and it booms out of each and every beach bar until late at night. Most of the clubs along *Slovenska obala* aim to attract party-goers.

WHERE TO STAY

The choice of hotels in Budva is one of the best in the whole country but it is a good idea – especially in the high season in July and August – to look for a place to stay in one of the smaller towns in the

Sundowners by the old town walls – this is the life on a balmy summer evening in Budva

vicinity or fall back on private accommodation to avoid the crowds.

APARTMENTS NEDOVIC-JAZ ✂

The personal alternative to the hotel: you can expect a friendly welcome; the apartments are simple and newly refurbished. The small kitchen is adequate for self-caterers and families. The view from the balcony is fabulous and the prices are extremely reasonable! *9 apartments | Lastva Grbaljska bb | mobile 067 59 06 55 | www.apartmentsnedovicjaz. com | Budget*

ASTORIA BUDVA ✂

A luxury hotel in an ideal location in the medieval old town. From the terraces you can enjoy the view over the rooftops and beaches of Budva. The roof terrace is magnificent. Prices in the low season are also slightly more reasonable. *6 rooms, 6 apartments. | Njegoševa 4 | tel. 033 45 11 10 | www.astoriamontenegro.com | Expensive*

AVALA ✂

The old Grand Hotel Avala was torn down and replaced by a new building with all the trimmings. The swimming pool is directly above the beach and the view of the bay and walls of the old town is impressive. But beware: this area is not exactly quiet at night. Breakfast is only available if you book half-board. *290 rooms | Mediteranska 2 | tel. 033 40 26 56 | www.avalaresort.com | Expensive*

INFORMATION

Mediteranska 8/6 | tel. 033 40 28 14 | www.budva.travel

WHERE TO GO

BEČIĆI (128 C5) (*ω M6*)

The residents here are proud of their 2 km/1.2 mi of beach that was voted the most beautiful in the Mediterranean. That was already 80 years ago, but does it matter? The coastal town (pop.

2,000) is located about 2 km/1.2 mi from Budva. Foreign investors have built luxurious hotels overlooking the beach – including spas and relaxation, caviar and lobster. Several travel organisations offer stays in these magnificent buildings at affordable prices. The ho-

sparesortbecici.com | Expensive) offers wellness and also bungee jumping.

PRŽNO (128 C6) *(𝄞 M6)*

It is also possible to spend wonderful sunny days in the appealing Bay of Pržno 3 km/1.9 mi further down the road along

A desire for luxury? In the Hotel Aman Sv. Stefan the view from the terrace and pool directly overlooks the sea

tels *Splendid (Expensive), Montenegro Beach Resort (Expensive)* and *Blue Star (Moderate–Expensive)* are part of the *Montenegrostars Hotel Group (tel. 033 77 37 77 | www.montenegrostars.com).* Tourists who can do without a lift that takes them straight from their room down to beach stay in one of the much more reasonably-priced private holiday apartments. *Stella di Mare (32 rooms | tel. 033 47 15 67 | Budget–Moderate)* on the other side of the coast road, is about 150 m/492 ft from the beach. It is small, welcoming and relatively reasonable. *The Spa Resort Bečići (20 apartments | Ive Lole Ribara | tel. 033 47 14 50 | www.*

the coast towards Petrovac and Ulcinj. A couple of *konobas* at the eastern end of the beach sweeten your stay. *The Maestral (171 rooms | tel. 033 41 01 00 | www. maestral.me | Expensive)* has one of the many hotel casinos that are especially popular with weekend tourists from Italy.

SV. STEFAN ★ (128 C6) *(𝄞 M6)*

Originally, the island measuring 4 acres was not connected to the mainland about 100 m/328 ft away. A promontory was not developed until the 19th century. This was supposed to make life easier for the fishermen on Sv. Stefan. However, the local fishermen were removed in 1956 and work started to convert it to a hotel island. The exterior of the 15th century village remained unchanged. But life inside the almost 100 stone houses was transformed into pure luxury. In 1960, the most expensive hotel opened in former Yugoslavia and it attracted many celebrities. Willy Brandt and Helmut Kohl, Claudia Schiffer and Silvester Stallone, Sophia Loren and Klaus Kinski came to Sv. Stefan. In 2009, the gem was sold. The investors came and went, and the hotel remained closed for a long while. The enchanted island with its red-roofed stone houses merely remained the most photographed symbol of Montenegro. The outlook from the ⇘ *viewing platform* on the main street of the "Pearl of the Adriatic" has certainly been captured millions of times.

After it was sold to a new owner and luxuriously renovated, the resort complex opened in 2013 as Hotel *Aman Sv. Stefan (50 rooms | tel. 033 42 00 00 | www.aman.com | Expensive)*. Its prices may be steep, but Sv. Stefan is regularly fully booked. The Serbian tennis star Novak Đoković got married in 2014 in the small island church and the photos were sent around the world. **INSIDER TIP** *Miločer*, the former summer residence of the Yugoslavian kings, which was built in the 1930s, is also part of the complex. The main residence is directly on a small bay, from the ⇘ restaurant terrace you can enjoy the view of Sv. Stefan. Other small houses are in a large park. The fragrance of cypress, oleander and pines accompany you on the way to your room.

Several restaurants are situated between Sv. Stefan and Miločer. Directly opposite the island, the ● *Olive (mobile 069 18 79 88 | www.olivetaste. com | Moderate–Expensive)* serves

Mediterranean cuisine, while in the evenings the terrace is particularly pleasant and welcoming. Not to worry, it doesn't get too expensive here. In Miločer Park in 2016 the renowned Japanese restaurant *Nobu (mobile 069 13 31 58 | www. noburestaurants.com | Expensive)* opened. Even if you don't want to stay or dine in Sveti Stefan and Miločer, you should at least enjoy a pleasant stroll here.

PETROVAC NA MORU

(129 D6) *(ⓜ N6)* **The tranquil little town ★ Petrovac na Moru (pop. 1,400) lies in a small bay directly beneath the coastal road that leads from Sv. Stefan to Sutomore and Bar.**

The settlement originally only consisted of a series of Venetian houses right on the bay – as na moru means "on the sea". The promenade has remained beautiful thanks to these houses that have been there for centuries. The forefathers of the inhabitants of Petrovac, who are members of the powerful Paštrovići clan, came down from the mountains above today's coast road where some of their stone houses have been preserved to this day.

Although there are many villas, apartments and small hotels in Petrovac, its location between the road and sea has to a large extent prevented the town from falling victim to the country's construction craze. Steps lead down to the water from the Medinski krš district shortening the distance to the town beach. However, it is much more pleasant to wander through the small alleys and breathe in the perfume of the Mediterranean plants. There are palm trees and cypresses at the beach and cafés, pubs and restaurants wait to welcome their guests not even 30 m/98.4 ft away. *The Caffe Cuba (Obala | mobile 069 03 43 63)*, which is decorated near the knuckle with pictures of Che Guevara and Fidel Castro in the interior, is a good place to relax and sip a Mojito or latte macchiato. You can settle down on one of the ● ⚲ old benches under the trees next to the beach. Who needs sun loungers on the beach itself that cost 10 euros a day? And you will still have the same view of the sea.

The two small *monasteries* in the town (14th and 15th century) are beautifully illuminated at night. There is a church on the island of *Sv. Neđelja* just off the coast; it is said that a sailor built it out of gratitude for having been rescued from the sea. There are daily boat excursions to the island.

As is the case with many other towns on the coast, Petrovac is also overcrowded during the high season. It is much more beautiful – and much less expensive – here in May and June when the broom bushes are in full bloom, or in September when the water is almost lukewarm.

SIGHTSEEING

KASTEL LASTVA

The waterside location on the western edge of the bay is already unique: the small fortress is a great destination for walks. *Free admission*

FOOD & DRINK

FORTUNA

What makes this restaurant so different from the others on the waterfront promenade, is not only the excellent food but also the "roof" of leaves of the rubber plants that flourish in the garden. There are also sea views. The first-rate fillet steak and pasta are highly recommended. *Obala | mobile 069 65 50 00 | www.facebook.com/ fortunapetrovac | Moderate*

LAZARET ⚲

This restaurant next to the fortress on the promenade serves very good pizza, lasagne and other quickly prepared meals. It is open until 2pm and the views are great! *Obala | mobile 069 02 61 57 | Budget*

INSIDER TIP ▶ PLAŽNI BAR MEDIN

A terrace, wooden tables, benches and chairs, drinks, good beer, sizeable portions of grilled meat on the plate, reasonable prices – and everything is very close to the beach. Too much to ask for? Not in this friendly restaurant that literally means "beach bar", but in fact is more a proper restaurant. *Lučice | mobile 069 45 63 80 | www.facebook.com/ medinbarpetrovac | Budget*

VILA CASTIO

Dana Đukovič-Kučko learned all there is to know about cooking and serving while working in a top hotel abroad. She returned to Petrovac almost 30 years later and opened her own restaurant on the promenade. She specialises in all kinds of fish and seafood. She also offers very pleasant guest rooms *(booking at www.booking.com). Obala | tel. 033 46 11 32 | Moderate*

BEACH

LUČICE

The shingles go on forever on the beach (250 m/820 ft long and 30 m/98.4 ft wide) on the eastern edge on the way out of town and just past the Hotel Rivijera. It is surrounded by two lovely, high green slopes.

WHERE TO STAY

PALAS

40 years ago it was already a flagship hotel for Western package-deal tourists. Now, you can book your own stay here. Spacious, tasteful and chic rooms with balconies and a swimming pool. The house is only separated from the sea by the coast road. *171 rooms | Obala | tel. 033 42 11 00 | Moderate*

PATAKI GUESTHOUSE ☼

Everything is taken care of – good and fairly priced. Situated slightly above the

is the friendly and helpful proprietors, Branka and Dragan. The five holiday apartments of different sizes – up to three rooms – are all well equipped, there are sea views from some of the large a terraces and barbecue facilities in the garden, as well as Wi-Fi and cable TV. *Medinski krš | tel. 033 46 18 79 | www. montenegro.ch | Budget–Moderate*

INFORMATION

Petrovac has no independent tourist office. Information is available at the office in Budva.

Atop of the rocks the Kastel Lastva watches over Petrovac na Moru and its bay

town, Pataki Guesthouse offers very spacious apartments with balconies and sea views. Outdoor pool. Friendly owners. *6 apartments | Buljarica bb | booking at www.booking.com | Budget*

INSIDER TIP ▶ VUKSANOVIĆ APARTMENTS

A special feature of this establishment

WHERE TO GO

BULJARICA ★ (129 E6) (*⊞ N6*)

2 km/1.2 mi south of Petrovac, this long stretch of bay is free of hotels – a rarity in Montenegro. The subterranean springs have prevented the development of Buljarica as it would be much too expensive to drain the ground. So

the 2 km/1.2 mi long beach gleams in the sunshine in all of its pristine glory. The eponymous village is located below the coastal road and is surrounded by lush greenery. If you book a stay here, you only have a ten minute walk to the beach. The restaurants are welcoming with friendly hosts and the prices are reasonable.

Studio Apartmani Đuković (mobile 069 81 00 03 | Budget) offers four inexpensive and very good holiday apartments. The camping site *Camping Maslina (mobile 068 60 20 40 | www.campingmaslina.com)*, is located in an olive grove near the sea. There are a few pubs and small guest houses right next to the water. Health is the top priority at the ● INSIDER TIP *Savojo Hotel (4 rooms, 4 apartments | mobile 067 22 14 42 | www.savojo.me | Moderate)*, also right on the coast: the owner is a practitioner

of sports medicine, his son a chiropractor and both offer physiotherapy programmes by the beach. They also serve 🌿 organic products and wine from their own cellar. The winds across the water change every hour and also contribute to one's physical wellbeing – they are great for your lungs!

SUTOMORE (130 A4) (𝄢 O7)
The name of the town (pop. 2,000, 13 km/8.1 mi from Petrovac) can be traced back to the Italian *sotto mare* and means "the lower sea". The long sandy beach remained unspoiled by tourism until two hotels opened their doors in the 1960s; most of the guests at the time were package holiday tourists who were not very demanding. The wind and water were sufficient to make them forget the shortcomings of the Socialist concrete buildings.

Today Sutomore has countless reasonably-priced accommodation options; there are small hotels and apartment houses all the way up to the coast road. However, you will only find peace and quiet higher up the mountain – as so often in Montenegro, the beach turns into one long disco at night and every pub plays its own kind of music at full volume. Instead of a hotel room, you should definitely book one of the attractive and reasonably priced private apartments here, for example, from *Apartments Abramovic (4 apartments | Blok Zelen | Obala Iva Novakovića | mobile 069 30 70 44 | booking at www.booking.com | Budget)*.

Saint Tekla church is an interesting cultural monument in Sutomore. An Orthodox and Catholic altar stand side by side as a sign of religious tolerance. The town is crowded in the summer months – especially on weekends when all of Podgorica migrates to the Adriatic coast.

ULCINJ (ULQIN)

(131 D6) *(🗺 R8)* **Nowhere else on the eastern Adriatic are the beaches as long and sandy as they are around Ulcinj (pop. 10,700), the southernmost town on the Montenegrin coast. In the town itself, you already feel as though you are in Albania.**

From time immemorial, the sea has washed sand ashore that is rich in salts; created by the erosion of quartz boulders, it reaches the coast with the flow of the Montenegrin Albanian border river, the Bojana.

Oriental flair pervades in every alley in Ulcinj. You notice it straight away – from the locals' busy activity and traditional dress, at the bazaar, the building style and the call of the Muezzin. Starting in the Middle Ages, migrants from the Slavic principality of Zeta settled here along with Albanians coming from the south who now make up more than three quarters of the population.

SIGHTSEEING

GRADSKI MUZEJ (CITY MUSEUM)

A piece of Turkey in Montenegro: stroll through an old Turkish prison and discover archaeological finds from antiquity like Muslim gravestones. *Mon–Fri 8am–8pm | at the western gate to the old town | www.ul-museum.me | admission 2 euros*

STARI GRAD (OLD TOWN) 🔆

You have to climb for a few minutes up steep paths, but it's worth it. The tiny narrow streets, partly renovated and partly ruined houses, the cyclopean walls of the old *citadel* – all these are testa-

Narrow alleys wind their way through Ulcinj's old town

ment to the rulers and inhabitants that changed down the centuries, the Illyrians, Greeks, Turks, Byzantines and Venetians. The *Balšić Tower (Balšića kula)* on the other hand was built in the days of the mediaeval state of Raška. And then there is the spectacular view of the coast!

FOOD & DRINK

Many Albanians have become successful restaurateurs, so it's up to you to choose between traditional Balkan cuisine (ćevapčići and ražnjići) and an excellent variety of fish in Ulcinj. No matter whether you select the ☆ *Aragosta (mobile 067 81 26 00 | Moderate–Expensive)* with a view of the harbour or *Antigona (mobile 069 53 35 91 | Moderate–Expensive)* in the old part of town or *Teuta (tel. 030 42 14 22 | Moderate–Expensive)* with its 1,400 ft² large terrace, you will be delighted by their excellent value for money. You can also eat well and inexpensively in the numerous bars and pizzerias at the Grand Beach, Velika plaža.

LEISURE & SPORTS

Ulcinj is an ideal location for surfers and kitesurfers because of the strong winds. Most facilities are at the grand beach. In the Bojana Delta the fishermen still cast their nets in the traditional way and you can be there to witness it.

BEACHES

CITY BEACHES

Gradska plaža, the city beach is also known as *Mala plaža* (the little beach) and is usually very crowded. There are several small beaches with deep water near the cliffs to the left of the sandy beach. A small nudist beach lies tucked away in the shade of some cypresses and there is also a very popular *ladies' beach* (*Ženska plaza*) where the sulphur, radium and sea salts are said to have healing properties.

VELIKA PLAŽA (GRAND BEACH) ★ ●

Copacabana and Tropicana are two major sections of the longest beach in Montenegro that stretches for more than 12 km/7.5 mi to the Albanian border. They are ideal for small children who can splash around in the shallow water.

WHERE TO STAY

Ulcinj promotes its large camping sites but they are rarely up to standard. Sometimes it is cheaper to opt for private accommodation; it is possible to pay less than 10 euros per night for a bed during the high season.

KULLA E BALSHAJVE ☆

The new, Albanian hotel owners in the old Balšić Tower have translated the name into their native language and added new furnishings to the small elegant hotel. The tower has a majestic view of the old town, the panoramic outlook is beautiful. *19 rooms | Stari grad | tel. 030 41 40 41 | www.hotelkullaebalshajve.com | Moderate–Expensive*

AGAINST THE CURRENT

When the large amount of water from the thaw of snow in the Albanian mountain regions makes the Bojana River's main tributary the Drim swell at the end of winter, the main river is no longer able to keep flowing in its customary direction.

Instead of flowing from Lake Skadar into the Adriatic, the river on the border of Montenegro and Albania starts to flow upstream. The fishermen who spread their trapeze nets in the Bojana Delta are then guaranteed fine catches!

LION

The Hotel Lion in Štoj – far away from the narrow streets of the old town of Ulcinj and surrounded by sand, the wind and the waves in the middle of the Grand Beach – will make you feel comfortable. *25 rooms | tel. 030 45 71 56 | www.hotel lion-ul.com | Moderate*

WHERE TO GO

ADA BOJANA (131 F6) *(ᗰ S8)*

The island in the delta of the Albanian Montenegrin border river 16 km/9.9 mi east of Ulcinj can only be reached from the mainland via a bridge. For everyone who likes to get back to nature –

In the Bojana Delta the fishmen still use these traditional suspended nets

INSIDER TIP ▶ VILA TAMARA

The owner Tamara Strugar personally takes care of her guests' wishes. The small house is located above the city beach and has a unique view over Old Ulcinj and the spectacular sunsets. The two apartments (which each accommodate up to six) are surrounded by a small garden full of agave and oleander. *Ivana Milutinovića | mobile 069 46 57 47 (June–Oct), tel. in Belgrade 00381 11 2 77 47 70 (Nov–May) | Budget*

INFORMATION

Đerđ Kastrioti Skenderberg bb | tel. 030 41 23 35 | www.ulcinj.travel

INSIDER TIP ▶ Montenegro's longest nudist beach is here.

There is not much choice of accommodation, but you will find a good place to stay just before the bridge at *Apartments Ada Bojana (3 apartments | Gornji Štoj | booking at www.booking.com | Budget)*.

On the island there are also camp sites. Despite or because of the modest infrastructure, Ada Bojana has developed into a paradise for tourists who are nature and sports enthusiasts.

The steady wind, the water and the sun also create ideal conditions for kite surfers. Further information is available at *www.kiteloop.net*

CETINJE, PODGORICA & LAKE SKADAR

The journey from Kotor to Cetinje offers one of the most beautiful views in Europe. You gain 1,000 m/3,281 ft in altitude in next to no time but negotiate about 30 hairpin bends enroute.

The incredible vista of the Bay of Kotor, which is surrounded by the karst formations of the Lovćen Mountains, opens up for all to see. There are also old roads from the north, from Nikšić, Danilovgrad or the Bosnian border and Grahovo leading to Cetinje. The more than a century old network of roads shows how important the city once was – and still is – for the residents of the region. It was the first capital of the new state established at the end of the 19th century after the freedom-loving Montenegrins had struggled against the Ottomans for centuries. Today, lively Podgorica is Montenegro's capital and at the same time its political, business and cultural centre.

Similar to the route over the Lovćen Mountains, the car ride on the old roads from Cetinje to Podgorica is another unforgettable highlight of any trip to Montenegro. Lake Skadar, down below on the plain, glitters in the sunlight in countless shades of green and dark blue. Hundreds of different birds nest around the largest lake on the Balkan Peninsula. Furthermore, the lake is an nearly inexhaustible source of food for the people living around it, who were almost completely cut off from the cities on the coast until a few decades ago, and lived off fishing.

Magnificent embassy buildings and quaint fishing villages: from the old capital to the shores of the largest lake in the Balkans

CETINJE

MAP INSIDE BACK COVER
(128 C3–4) (*L–M4*) **The histori-cal capital city ★ Cetinje (pop. 14,000) feels like a large open air museum.**

A city full of traces of the years after the first independence of Montenegro following the 1878 Congress of Berlin: embassies of all of the major powers of the time, who maintained contacts to King Nikola I, are scattered throughout the town. The king craftily saw that his daughters married into the courts of many of the continent's royal fami-lies and, in this way, made the small country more influential than it would ever be again. The history of the com-munity, built on a barren field of karst, dates back to the 15th century when the first Montenegrin ruler, Ivan Crnojević, established his residence here while retreating from the Turks. The spiritual and political leader had the monastery in Cetinje built in 1484. At the end of the

19th century the sleepy artists' metropolis was given the new appearance that it has retained to this day: low houses and straight streets lined with lime trees and acacias.

SIGHTSEEING

Cetinje's top attraction is not the bricks and mortar but the historic atmosphere of this small city. So, put on your sturdy evening in the low floodlighting. It's not surprising that it was a model for the Montenegrin royal family's other palaces. Today, this is the elegant headquarters of the Ministry of Culture.

Just around the corner is the inconspicuous *Vlah Church (Vlaška crkva | Baja Pivljanina)* from 1450, the city's oldest building. The church is named after the cattle herders who once grazed their cattle here. According to legend, under

These walls guard the national epic and a famous billiard table: Biljarda

hiking boots and set off on a walking tour! Among the *old embassy buildings* from the independence era is the impressive architecture of the most important European powers back then – Russia *(Vuka Mićunovića)*, England *(Trg Novice Cerovića)*, Austria-Hungary *(Pivljanina)* and France *(Njegoševa)*. Just opposite the French embassy is the splendid *Blue Castle (Plavi Dvorac | Njegoševa)*. The former residence of Crown Prince Danilo, which is in the middle of the city park, not only looks magnificent in the the tombstones in front of the church are the mortal remains of the infamous robber chief Bajo Pivljanin and his wife. Take a stroll in Baja Pivljanina towards the south-east. The white *Royal Theatre (Zetski Dom | V Proleterske Brigade)* with its entrance pillars once housed all kinds of things: a museum, library and theatre. Today, you can only admire it from the outside. On the nearby square Dvorski Trg is the small, beautiful *Court Church (Crkva na Ćipuru)* which was constructed in 1886 on the ruins of the historic monastery. King Nikola I and Queen Milena are buried here.

At the city's central museum administration in the *Government House (Vladin dom)* tourists can buy discount combitickets (10 euros) for the Montenegrin Art Gallery, the King Nikola Museum and the History Museum. The opening times of all the museums are (unless otherwise stated below): *April–Oct Mon–Sat 9am–5pm, Nov–March 9am–4pm | www.mnmuseum.org*

BILJARDA (NJEGOŠ MUSEUM)

The former residence of the poet Prince Bishop Petar Njegoš includes books from his library and his own writings – including the manuscript of "The Mountain Wreath" – as well as the billiard table that was to give the building its name. It was transported on donkeyback up the stony road from Kotor at the beginning of the 19th century. *Trg Novice Cerovića | admission 3 euros*

CRNOGORSKA GALERIJA UMJETNOSTI MIODRAG DADO ĐURIĆ (ART GALLERY)

The former Trgopromet department store, a linear building and showpiece of socialist architecture now displays the country's modern art in all its genres: sculpture and fine arts, happenings, performances, digital and intermedia works. The gallery was named after the most famous Montenegrin painter Dado Đurić. *April–Oct. Tue–Sun 10am–2pm, 5pm–9pm, Nov–March Tue–Sat 10am–5pm | Njegoševa | admission 4 euros*

MUZEJ KRALJA NIKOLE (KING NIKOLA MUSEUM)

The castle has been a museum since 1926: the ruler's parade, hunting and trophy weapons are displayed on the ground floor. A tour of the first floor, with the living quarters and work rooms

decorated with the original furniture and paintings, gives an impression of the everyday life of King Nikola. *Trg Novice Cerovića | admission 5 euros*

UMJETNIČKI MUZEJ CRNE GORE (ART MUSEUM)

The collection of Yugoslavian and Montenegrin art dates back to the 17th century. The highlight is the *Icon of Mary the Mother of God by Philernmos*, the patron saint of the Order of Knights of St John, that is displayed in the Blue Chapel. The golden portrait is one of the most important sacred relics of Christianity. It is said that it was painted by Luke the Evangelist. *Novice Cerovića | admission 4 euros*

FOOD & DRINK

BELVEDER ☽

This restaurant that first opened its doors as a coffee house in 1888, boasts

★ **Cetinje**
The old capital city with the historic embassies is like an enormous open air museum → p. 65

★ **Njegoš Mausoleum**
The view from the country's major attraction stretches across the Adriatic as far as Italy → p. 68

★ **Njeguši**
The air-dried ham from this village is famous worldwide → p. 69

★ **Skadarsko jezero (Lake Skadar)**
Countless species of birds and an abundance of fish – a treasure trove of nature's riches → p. 72

MARCO POLO HIGHLIGHTS

CETINJE

You should not miss out on this speciality: the famed Njeguši ham

panoramic views from the terrace that sweep across Lake Skadar as far as Albania. You should try the tasty lamb cooked under the sač. *Magistralni put E 80 bb | tel. 067 56 92 17 | Budget*

RESTAURANT KOLE

Here, you can relax after visiting the old capital's historic sites. Quick service, appetizing, not too expensive, very friendly and with a fun design – and mainly popular with locals. What more can you want? The cuisine at Restaurant Kole is very meaty, but it tastes great. *Bulevar Crnogorskih Junaka 12 | mobile 069 60 66 60 | Moderate*

WHERE TO GO

NJEGOŠ MAUSOLEUM ★ ● ☀
(128 B4) (⊠ L4–5)
Take a deep breath and get ready to climb the never-ending steps! On the second highest summit in the Lovćen Mountains, the Jezerski vrh (1,660 m/ 5,446 ft), Montenegro's poet prince, Njegoš, lies buried in an oversized mausoleum. It is flanked by two giant black marble statues of women and an equally imposing statue of Njegoš. A mosaic made from 20,000 gilt pieces decorates the ceiling inside. From Njeguši a signposted hiking path leads to the mountain, in the *Lovćen National Park*. The ascent lasts around four hours and the return hike approx. three-and-a-half hours. By car you drive to the summit from Cetinje for 20 km/12.4 mi on a narrow, tarmac serpentine road. When you arrive, you must still climb up 461 steps to the mausoleum before you can enjoy the magnificent view over Montenegro. Enjoy the wonderful panoramic view – over the Bay of Kotor, Lake Skadar and as far as Albania! *May–Sept daily 8am– 6pm | admission 3 euros*

NJEGUŠI ★ (128 A4) (*L4*)

In the birthplace of the poet and Prince Petar Njegoš, 23 km/14.3 mi west of Cetinje, smoked products are still very popular: the ham from Njeguši (pop. 200) is famous far beyond the boundaries of Montenegro. You can also buy smoked cheese, wine and home-distilled spirits – look for the signs (pršut, sir, vino, rakija). The house Njegoš was born in is only open in summer and can be found – there is a signpost – on the main road. ⌇ *Kod Pera Na Bukovicu (tel. 069 05 50 21 | www.kodpera.com | Budget–Moderate)*, the oldest pub in the region, serves all of the local specialities – and also guarantees a spectacular view of the Lovćen.

OBOD (129 D4) (*N5*)

On a small hill opposite Rijeka Crnojevića, 18 km/11.2 mi from Cetinje there is an Orthodox church and a few old stone houses, but you will hardly see any people. For Montenegrins, this seemingly inconspicuous place (pop. 200) has great historic importance. In 1475, Prince Ivan Crnojević and his entourage escaped from the Turks by retreating from Lake Skadar to Obod. Only a few years after Johannes Gutenberg had invented book printing, his son Đurađ established the first printing press in south-east Europe here in the year 1493; it was later transferred to Cetinje. The first book to be printed in Cyrillic letters was produced in Obod.

RIJEKA CRNOJEVIĆA (129 D3) (*N4*)

Those who take the old road from Cetinje to Podgorica will be rewarded with spectacular views of Lake Skadar. The river – which is also named *Rijeka Crnojevića* – with its beautiful green water winds its way into the lake. The small village, 16 km/9.9 mi outside Cetinje, at first sight makes a curious impression

with its ruined buildings scattered all around. But don't be put off! The tiny centre with the old, incredibly steep and charming stone bridge is beguiling. You can eat well in the restaurant named *Mostina (mobile 069 84 33 17 | Moderate–Expensive)*.

PODGORICA

⬚ MAP INSIDE BACK COVER

(124 C5) (*O2*) **In the early evening at the very latest, it will become clear where the heartbeat of the capital city (pop. 186,000) can be felt: all cars are banned from the zone between Freedom Street (Slobode) and Marka Miljanova after 5pm.**

After that, the area near the Parliament and National Theatre belongs to those out for a stroll. And anybody who stays longer, and is not only passing through, soon learns to take a second look at things. Podgorica is not among the pearls of European capitals, as there are not enough top attractions. But the spacious parks, lively shopping streets and

---

CITY WHERE TO START?

Trg Republike: Independence Square is in the middle of the city centre on Slobode street. From the airport, it takes you about 5 minutes by car to get here. There are shops and shopping centres all around, where you have a good chance of finding a parking space. Bulevar Svetog Petra Cetinjskog and its magnificent parks are only a few minutes' walk. Another 400 m/1,312 ft further on, you already reach the Osman clock tower Sahat kula in the historic old town.

two rivers flowing through the middle Morača and Ribnica make the small capital interesting. The city in the fertile Zeta Valley was first mentioned by the name of Ribnica *(riba = fish)*. Podgorica ("at the foot of the hill") was renamed in 1326. To honour the special commitment of Montenegrin partisans, it was given the name of Titograd during Yugoslavia's Socialist period before finally reverting to its old name in 1992.

SIGHTSEEING

CENTAR SAVREMENE UMJETNOSTI (CENTRE FOR CONTEMPORARY ART) ●

Do you feel like a change from the old favourites? Then this museum is perfect for you. It is housed in the old winter palace of King Nikola in the Kruševac park on the Morača River where the Gallery of the Nonaligned States was housed until 1985. And even today, paintings from Montenegro and the other republics of former Yugoslavia still hang on the walls alongside works by artists from Bolivia, Egypt and Cuba. *Mon–Fri 9am–2pm and 4pm–9pm | Kruševac bb | free admission*

GORICA ☆

From the northern hill there is a fantastic view of the Morača with the *Millenium Bridge* and the stadium of the FK Budućnost (which means "future") Podgorica football club and you will also be able to take a look inside the 12th century church *Sv. Đorđe (Saint George)*.

SABORNI HRAM HRISTOVOG VASKRSENJA (CATHEDRAL OF THE RESURRECTION OF CHRIST)

It was only just built and is already a city landmark: the Serbian Orthodox Cathedral with its almost 36 m/118.1 ft high dome and stone façade designed to

London on the Morača River? Podgorica makes a modern impression thanks to its Millennium Bridge

look old was only consecrated in 2013. It is Montenegro's largest orthodox church. Take a look inside, it's well worth it! *Bulevar Džordža Vašingtona 3*

STARA VAROŠ

The Ribnica River forms the boundary between the new *(nova)* and old *(stara)* sections of Podgorica. The days of Ottoman rule come back to life when one hears the Muezzin calling the faithful to prayer in the Stara Varoš quarter. The clock tower from the 17th century, *Sahat kula* on *Trg Bećir Bega Osmanagića Square*, is one of the few well-preserved examples of Islamic architecture in Podgorica.

FOOD & DRINK

INSIDER TIP **KUŽINA** ●

If someone is bold enough to call his restaurant the "kitchen", then it must be good! It offers traditional dishes: lamb roasted under the red-hot ceramic lid, or sač, goat from the grill, Montenegrin polenta and all kinds of sweet desserts are some of the specialities. *Trg Božane Vučinić 2 | tel. 020 63 38 33 | Budget–Moderate*

INSIDER TIP **MANTRA** ❀

Indian cuisine from breakfast to dinner, a small garden, brightly coloured sofas and cushions in Indian textiles, Indian music – you almost forget that you are in Montenegro. Vegetarians and vegans will feel at home here. The Mantra has also a delivery service that even comes to your hotel room. *Ivana Milutinovića 21 | tel. 020 242888 | www.mantrapodgorica.com | Budget*

ENTERTAINMENT

When the heat of day has finally become less stifling, the capital springs back to life in the magical square between Stanka Dragojevića, Karađorđeva, Slobode and Hercegovačka. This is where you will find the most bars and pubs of Podgorica; they cater to all tastes from the rustic beer hall *Pivnica (Stanka Dragojevića 12)*, to the hip *Buda Bar (Stanka Dragojevića 26)*. At the ● *Kino Kultura (Proleterske Brigade 1)* foreign films are usually shown in English with Serbian subtitles.

LANTERNA PODGORICA

The name "lantern" sounds cosy enough – and it doesn't promise too much, especially if you like the stone and wood furnishings. In the evenings, things really take off here – often with live music late into the night. And you can also order food – served all day: usually hearty, always delicious and at very reasonable prices. Excellent house wines and beers. *Marka Miljanova 41 | tel. 020 663163*

WHERE TO STAY

There is a wide selection of business hotels as many international companies and foreign embassies have offices in Podgorica. There are also numerous reasonably-priced apartments – most of them in the city centre. For example, the operators of a bed and breakfast hotel, the *Piramida (10 rooms | Ul. Nikole Tesle 26 | tel. 020 611608 | www.hotelpiramida.me | Moderate)*, a little way out of town, also offer well-equipped apartments in the centre (*Budget*). *The Apartman Vanja (Bulevar Save Kovačevića 145 | booking at www.booking.com | Budget–Moderate)* is a mini-apartment (about 375 ft²) with kitchen, balcony and full amenities.

KERBER

This hotel is wonderfully tucked away in the heart of the city but still only a two minute walk from the hustle and bustle on the chic shopping street Sloboda. It radiates the charm of the old days, but it's still very good value for money. *20 rooms | Novaka Miloševa 6 | tel. 020 40 54 05 | www.hotelkerber.me | Moderate*

INFORMATION

Ul. Slobode 67 | tel. 020 66 75 35 | www. podgorica.travel

WHERE TO GO

DUKLIJA (124 C5) *(𝄢 O2)*
The first Illyrian city conquered by the Romans is only 3 km/1.9 mi north of Podgorica, near the village of Rogami, the ruins include traces of an ancient sewage system along with the stone remains of baths and a basilica.

BIRD LAND

Montenegro's diverse countryside attracts a rich variety of bird species that is unrivalled in Europe. On Lake Skadar alone almost 300 different bird species flock and a quarter-of-a-million birds from northern Europe have their winter quarters in this region. Pelicans are equally at home on the lake as well as Europe's second biggest cormorant colony. Bird-watching tours are organised here and in Biogradska Gora National Park, in Durmitor National Park, where ornithologists have discovered more than 100 species, or in the marshlands around Ulcinj. For more information please go to *short.travel/mon9*.

INSIDER TIP **ŠIPČANIK** (124 C6) *(𝄢 P3)*
10 km/6.2 mi south of the capital, on the 5,600-acre Čamovsko polje the best wines of Montenegro are grown. The wine estate Plantaže has a giant wine cellar 30 m/98.4 ft below ground that is open to visitors. You can also take a tour of the vineyards: a miniature train transports you across the plain among millions of vines. Alongside the local varieties Vranac (red) and Krstač (white) some excellent Sauvignon, Chardonnay or Cabernet grapes ripen in Montenegro's sunshine. *Wine tasting 10–30 euros | www.plantaze.com*

SKADARSKO JEZERO (LAKE SKADAR)

(130–131 A–F 1–3) *(𝄢 N–S 3–6)* **Gardens covered in vines, dilapidated churches in the valley and white-walled cemeteries set in lush meadows and fertile fields: the residents of ★ Lake Skadar live in harmony with nature and reap the benefits of its bounty.**

For centuries, rebellious Montegrin clans and Turkish conquerors fought over this body of water. Today, the border between Montenegro and Albania runs down the middle of the lake, which is named after the most important city on its shores Skadar (Albanian: Shkoder). It is fed by subterranean springs and has the same temperature throughout the year even though the ice-cold water of the *Morača* flows into it on the west side. The lake is the largest on the Balkan Peninsula. After the snow thaw in spring, it expands to cover an area of more than 190 mi^2 and is still over 115 mi^2 in autumn. Its wealth of fish and great variety

Nature paradise on Lake Skadar: who still wants to visit the Adriatic now?

of birdlife are unequalled in Europe and make it a paradise for nature lovers.

In 1983 Montenegro realised that this habitat was worth protecting and part of the lake was declared a national park. The Albanian section has also been protected since 2005.

You should definitely visit this unique natural habitat. Your (digital) photo album will reap the rewards: ibises and storks gather in the shallow water, the surface of the lake is covered with water lilies and other rare plants and glitters in many colours. There is a wonderful fragrance from the laurel trees on the lake shores and the chestnut trees soar up to the skies. The *Rijeka Crnojevića* river its winds its way fjord-like to the lake. Old fishing villages and convents where nuns dressed in black carry out their work in silence are the kinds of scenes from a world that is no more than two hours away from all of the hustle and bustle of the tourist towns on the coast.

INFORMATION

Lake Skadar Visitors Centre | Mon–Sat 9am–3pm | Virpazar | tel. 020 87 91 03 | npskadarskojezero@nparkovi.me

WHERE TO GO ON LAKE SKADAR

BEŠKA ● (130 C2–3) (*M P–Q6*)

Swallows, snakes and stones – that was what constituted the tiny island in the southern part of Lake Skadar until 2004. Then Orthodox nuns arrived and settled in the convent that had been deserted for 300 years. They have had electricity for a few years now but there is still no running water. The barren island smells of rosemary and sage, the sun burns down and the nuns work and pray until late at night. And, they welcome day-trippers who bring some change to their monotonous life. Two and eight hour boat trips are offered locally. Most of the excursion and mosques next to each other – many of the Albanian residents here are Catholic. The village is slightly higher up in the mountains. Accommodation and restaurants are directly by the lake. The route Virpazar–Murići also serves as a cycle path, and you can find out more information in the visitor's centre in Virpazar.

PLAVNICA (130 A–B1) (*∭ P4*)

An ultra-modern hotel complex *(Plavnica Eco Resort | 4 apartments | tel. 020 44 3700 | www.plavnica.me | Expensive)* has been built in the village of Plavnica on the north bank of Lake Skadar. The luxurious apartments are named after the last Montenegrin princesses. From the futuristic terrace, hotel guests have a view across the large swimming pool to the lake. The resort is also an event location: concerts, fashion shows and beauty contests are held here.

VIRPAZAR (129 E–F5) (*∭ O5*)

Tourists will immediately see that the largest town (pop. 1,000) on the Montenegrin shore of Lake Skadar held a strategically important position for centuries. It was once an island – and the last bastion against the Turks. If you follow the dead-straight railway embankment that was built in the 1970s for a mile or so towards Podgorica, you will see the Lesendra fortress (free admission) on the left-hand side. The Turkish stronghold was built to secure the conquests of the pashas in Istanbul. Today, two bridges connect the fishing village with the coast.

From the end of April, when iris and water lilies are in full bloom, the boat excursion season for private hire begins among the reeds by the lake shore. You will notice that you're in a wonderful location at the latest after your arrival when you meet a group of friendly

Once strategically important, today a leisure site: Virpazar on Lake Skadar

boats depart from Virpazar or Murići in the morning. Information is available from the Visitor Centre in Virpazar.

MURIĆI (130 B3) (*∭ P6*)

Do you have a head for heights? From Virpazar a winding road leads through the mountains into the village. The area that you are travelling through looks like a moon landscape and Skadar Lake glimmers to the left of the route. After Murići the road continues over Mount Rumija (1,584 m/5,197 ft) to Ulcinj and Ada Bojana. Similar to other villages in this region, Murići has Catholic churches locals offering you "the best" boat excursions. Take your time and compare the prices at leisure before you choose. The weekly market that gave the village its name (Virpazar means "lively market") is held on Friday and is full of colour. In a babble of Montenegrin and Albanian, peasant women and fishermen offer delicacies of the area from fresh oil to carp to tomatoes and peppers. You can even collect some natural products yourself near Virpazar. If you drive in the direction of Rijeka Crnojevića and leave the main road for a short while, close by you will find ● plenty of wild herbs such as sage, rosemary and thyme. Pleasant accommodation is available at the *Guesthouse Vukasevic (4 rooms | booking at www.booking.com | Moderate)* in a central location on the main square: welcoming, family-friendly and first-class!

ŽABLJAK (130 A1) (*𝄞 O4*)

It is possible that the myth of Montenegro's Black Mountain has its origins in this sleepy little village 23 km/14.3 mi from Virpazar. Before the Ottomans started making life difficult for the founder of the state Ivan Crnojević and his companions, they had their ancestral seat in this fortress on the edge of Lake Skadar – it was a safe haven in the midst of the hostility of nature. However, after the Turkish troops had conquered Podgorica and Skadar, the members of the Crnojević clan saw themselves forced to give up their vulnerable retreat on the plain and move to highlands of Obod and Cetinje at the end of the 15th century. A trail leads up to the well-preserved ✄ INSIDERTIP castle ruins (free admission) in 15 minutes. From the top there is a magnificent view of the landscape – especially after the snow thaw in spring when the flowers are in full bloom. A

memorial stone on the north-west wall commemorates the battle of 1835 that drove the Turks out of the village.

LEISURE & SPORTS

Hikers and cyclists follow the 3.5 km/ 2.2 mi long *art tour*: a series of works by Montenegrin sculptors on the millers' path between the two villages of Poseljani and Smokovci. You can extend the tour as far as Rijeka Crnojevića. There is also a *wine route* between Virpazar and Rijeka. Anglers and bird lovers can explore the lake by boat. The visitor centres in Vranjina, Murići and Rijeka Crnojevića provide local information. In Virpazar, plenty of boat excursion tours are also on offer. The visitors' centre in town also rents hiking equipment.

LOW BUDGET

In Montenegro, the summer sales last from June to August. Department stores such as *Delta City (Cetinjski put | www.deltacity.me) and Mall of Montenegro (Bulevar Save Kovačevića 74 | www.mallof montenegro.com)* in Podgorica offer brand-name articles at greatly reduced prices during this time.

The village of Medun north-east of Podgorica is considered the "capital" of the Kuči clan, which produced many freedom fighters. The poet Marko Miljanov documented the history of the clan during the 19th century and the museum *(daily 9am–7pm| free admission)* in his former residence provides information on his life and the Kučis.

THE NORTH-WEST

More than 20 mountain peaks over 2,000 m/6,562 ft high, more than a dozen glacial lakes and countless springs, brooks and rivers: when you set off to explore the pristine beauty of the Montenegrin mountain region, you should plan to visit the area between Žabljak and Nikšić in the north-west.

The Durmitor National Park offers mountaineers a wide selection of routes – and, in winter, the ski slopes provide some of the best downhill runs on the Balkan Peninsula. A rafting trip on the Tara, the wild river of the north, has become something of a must for all visitors to Montenegro. A feast for the eyes at any time of the year: the Black Lake (Crno jezero) near Žabljak and the Ledena pećina (Ice cave) with its stalactites and stalagmites.

NIKŠIĆ

(124 B4) (♨ U13) The second largest city in Montenegro (pop. 72,000) has always been overshadowed historically by Podgorica and Cetinje.

But don't give up: a castle, fortress and important church are already a good start. Then, there are the splendid destinations in the vicinity especially Ostrog Monastery!

Although Nikšić was known as "the city of steel and beer" during the Tito era, not much remained of the steel industry after the Yugoslavian Wars and hardly anybody drank the famous Nikšićko pivo that had been brewed here since 1896. It was not until the

The area with the deepest gorges and highest mountains: untamed Montenegro awaits in the Durmitor Mountains and Tara Canyon

state-run brewery was sold that things started to look up and the unemployment rate decreased.

SIGHTSEEING

SV. VASILIJE OSTROŠKI (ST VASILIJE CHURCH)
The church next to the Royal Palace already dazzles in white from a far distance. It was erected in honour of the soldiers who lost their lives in the battle against the Turks in 1878.

UTVRĐENJE (FESTUNG)
The approx. 200 m/656 ft long, well-preserved fortress at the western entrance to Nikšić was erected by the Ottoman rulers in the 16th century. Enjoy a leisurely stroll and in summer the free music and theatre at open-air events. *Free admission*

ZAVIČAJNI MUZEJ GRADA NIKŠIĆA (REGIONAL MUSEUM)
Not bad for a local heritage museum: it is housed in a real palace – and a very

beautiful one. In the old days this was the residence of King Nikola, and his reign is also the focal point of the exhibition. *Daily 10am–1pm, 5pm–8pm | Trg Šaka Petrovića 1 | admission 2 euros*

FOOD & DRINK

There are many small pubs and bistros in the centre of town. Apart from

tel. 040 213766 | www.facebook.com/ forestniksic | Budget–Moderate

WHERE TO STAY

APARTMENTS DRAGOVIĆ NIKŠIĆ

What are you looking for in Nikšić? Spacious apartments, friendly, helpful hosts with plenty of tips for excursions and rafting tours, close to the centre and an

Hewn into the rocks, the Ostrog Monastery is considered sacred by Orthodox, Catholics and Muslims alike

them, the few good restaurants are found in the hotels such as the Trim and Trebjesa.

FOREST CAFÉ & LOUNGE BAR

In central Montenegro people also move with the times: the Forest is now called "Café & Lounge Bar". You will feel relaxed here from breakfast to a late night sundowner. Delicious dishes are the *ćevapčići* (type of kebab) and *pljeskavica* (burgers). *Ivana Milutinovića |*

excellent breakfast? Bingo – you'll find everything here! *3 apartments | Serdara Scepana bb | tel. 040 200600 | www. apartmanidragovicniksic.com | Moderate*

TREBJESA

This small hotel (newly elaborately renovated) lies a short way away from the city centre but this is compensated for by its idyllic location in a pine forest. *8 rooms | Trebjesa | tel. 077 20 00 60 | www.hoteltrebjesa.me | Budget–Moderate*

Ivana Milutinovića 10 | tel. 040 212511 | www.niksic.travel

WHERE TO GO

MANASTIR OSTROG ★ ●
(124 C4) (*ጠ U13*)

At first glance, the walls of the small room where the body of Saint Vasilije is preserved looks like they are covered in tattoos: frescoes of the saints have been painted directly on to the stone as one last sign of respect for the builder of the monastery. In 1665, the then Metropolitan of Herzegovina, Vasilije Ostrovski had the white building hewed into the rock after he had fled from the Turks and been forced to abandon his ancestral seat further to the west.

Later the sanctuary, which is located 22 km/13.7 mi away from Nikšić, became an important place of pilgrimage for believers from all parts of devotion and Yugoslavia. Many Orthodox families still have their children christened here. Even Catholics and Muslims consider the place holy.

Be careful: the road that leads up to Ostrog is steep and winding! First, you arrive at the lower monastery, then there is a steep climb to the spectacular upper monastery hewn into the rock. From the car park it is another ten minute walk. You need about 45 minutes to walk all the way from the lower to upper monastery.

The motel INSIDER TIP *Koliba Bogetići (mobile 067 88 81 89 | www.kolibe.me | Budget–Moderate)* is only 8 km/5 mi south on the road towards Podgorica. The traditional food there is excellent, the service friendly and the fresh air invigorating.

ŽABLJAK

(124 C2) (*ጠ V12*) **The highest town (at 1,450 m/4,757 ft) in Montenegro is also a centre of mountain tourism and winter sports – with many ideal excursion destinations in the immediate vicinity.**

Although Žabljak was destroyed several times during the Second World War, the typical mountain houses with their steep roofs still make this small town (pop. 2,000) a charming place to visit. But when the early morning mist rises from the Black Lake and disappears between the peaks of the Bobotov kuk and the other mountains (over 2,000 m/6,562 ft high), it is hard to believe that people have ever put foot here.

★ **Manastir Ostrog**
The white monastery in the rocks is an important sanctuary for Orthodox Christians → p. 79

★ **Durmitor Nacionalni Park**
Unspoiled nature at an altitude of more than 2,000 m/6,562 ft: Durmitor is the most beautiful national park in Montenegro → p. 81

★ **Manastir Piva**
The walls of this mediaeval monastery are decorated with countless frescoes → p. 82

★ **Tara**
Be carried away by the rapids on a rafting trip through the deepest canyon in Europe → p. 83

MARCO POLO HIGHLIGHTS

FOOD & DRINK

KRCMA NOSTALGIJA

The name "Nostalgia Guesthouse" says it all: no gourmet cuisine, but hearty, typical Montenegrin food in a cosy atmosphere and also a few tables outside. The staff are friendly, and there are also several ⊛ vegetarian choices. *Vuka Karadžića | mobile 069 63 06 96 | Budget*

SHOPPING

INSIDER TIP Products from the mountain region, as well as shoes and clothing from all over the world, are sold in the indoor daily market. ⊛ On the ground floor farmers from the nearby villages sell cheese, potatoes and herbs, and even thick home-made pullovers (using wool from their own sheep) until the early afternoon.

LEISURE & SPORTS

In winter, you have no other option other than getting out on the slopes.

LOW BUDGET

Keep your eyes open for farmers selling sheep and goats cheese at the farmers' markets! The prices are especially low here.

At the ☀ Guest House Nena (4 rooms | Selo Kovacka dolina bb | mobile 067 63 80 87 | booking at www.booking.com), a few miles from the centre of Žabljak, you can stay very cheaply and enjoy the friendly and cosy atmosphere. Plus, the views are spectacular.

Seven ski lifts covering an area of 3,900 m/12,795 ft are in constant use, a day pass costs approx. 15 euros. In summer you can book rafting tours, jeep safaris, mountain biking, canyoning excursions and paragliding, as well as horseback rides and angling trips, hikes or eco tour offers. The majestic, unspoiled natural landscape of the northwest is unique and offers ideal conditions for all these activities. There is a wide choice of tour operators and all work with exceptional local guides with expert knowledge of the region. The prices are comparable. *Eco-Tours (Dunje Ðokić | mobile 067 25 90 20 | www.eco-tours.co.me)* has its offices in Kolašin in the north-east, but also has the best offers for the northwestern region of the country.

WHERE TO STAY

AUTOCAMP RAZVRŠJE

Those who do not want to spend the night in their own tent on the camping site can opt for one of the rustic huts. The mother of the owner Mišo Vojinović bustles about in the kitchen where she ● ⊛ bakes bread and cooks meals for the campers using everything fields and meadows have to offer. Vojinović also offers a variety of tours for his guests. *Mobile 067 44 44 77 | Budget–Moderate*

GUEST HOUSE DURMITOR PARADISE

Centrally located and an ideal starting point for hiking tours. The very friendly and committed host offers a superb breakfast. However, some rooms are very small. *4 rooms | Sinjajevinska bb | mobile 067 35 38 78 | www.durmitorparadise.com | Budget–Moderate*

HOTEL SOA ☀

Everything is perfect here. One of the new residential glass and granite

Hold the reins, let go of your everyday routine: riding holiday near Žabljak

complexes built by private investors in Žabljak. Chic design, modern furnishings and an uninterrupted view of the Durmitor Mountains guarantee guests a pleasant stay. *18 rooms | Nacionalni Park Durmitor | tel. 052 36 0110 | www.hotel soa.com | Expensive*

INFORMATION

Trg Durmitorskih ratnika 3 | tel. 052 36 18 02 | www.tozabljak.com

WHERE TO GO

DURMITOR NACIONALNI PARK ★
(124–125 B–D 2–3) *(∅ U–W 11–12)*

In 1980 Durmitor National Park was declared a Unesco World Heritage Site. Its area of 150 mi^2 offers all that you've ever desired: deep canyons, high mountains, caves, glacial lakes and a boundless variety of flora and fauna. The area around Žabljak alone has around 1,300 species of plants and it is also a paradise for bird lovers.

The park extends over a high plateau at an altitude of around 1,500 m/4,921 ft with even higher peaks rising up – the highest is the Bobotov kuk with 2,522 m/8,274 ft. Climbers have five huts at their disposal as well as accommodation options in Škarka, Šušica, at the Sedlo mountain saddle and some limited possibilities in Lokvice and Velika Kalica. You can spend the night in cosy peasant huts at the *Black Lake (Crno jezero)* in summer and winter and rent private rooms locally. The *national park information centre (Ul. Jovana Cvijića | Žabljak | tel. 052 36 02 28 | npdurmitor@nparkovi.me)* provides further information. For all those who don't want to overdo the climbing, there is a picturesque hiking route around the lake, which you can easily walk in one or two hours.

There is a demanding hike from Žabljak to the Bobotov kuk that takes around seven hours. The path begins 3 km/1.9 mi outside of the village at Crno jezero, where a signpost indicates the marked route to *Indjini Dolovi*. After

Enjoy a unique view of Tara Bridge during a rafting tour

approx. four hours of hiking through karst craters and scree, you arrive at the *Ledena pećina (Ice Cave)* at an altitude of more than 2,000 m/6,562 ft. There is a further steep path up to the ☆ *Velika Previja*, lookout point where you can refresh yourself at a spring. And then, it is only another 45 minutes to the peak of the Bobotov kuk. You can make the downward hike from Velika Previja via

Zeleni Vir and *Urdeni Do* to *Dobri Do* or the mountaineers' house in *Sedlo*.

MANASTIR PIVA ★ (124 B2) *(ⓜ U12)*

Piva Monastery (55 km/34.2 mi from Žabljak) has a chequered history: in order to prevent the 16th century three-nave church falling victim to the dam being constructed in Plužine, people began dismantling it bit by bit and rebuilding it at its current location in 1969. This action took just as long as the initial construction of the church. The walls are covered with frescoes; the paintings cover an area of more than 10,700 ft². Pay particular attention to the INSIDER TIP fresco over the south entrance: unique in Orthodox churches, it shows a picture of the Turkish Pasha Mehmed Sokolović, a relative of the Serbian patriarch at the time who had converted to Islam.

PLJEVLJA (124–125 C–D1) *(ⓜ V11)*

Many visitors don't manage to get this far – the north-westerly tip of Montenegro. But you should definitely visit! The tour to Žabljak (pop. 19,000) about 60 km/37.3 mi away is well worth it. Not only to admire the town's landmark – the *Hussein Pasha Mosque (Husein pašina džamija)*, with its tall slender minaret was erected shortly after the Turkish conquest in the 16th century – but also to explore the traces of ancient Illyrian and Roman settlements in the vicinity. Archaeologists found the remains of a Roman town near the hamlet of *Komine* but were only able to decipher the first letter of its name. The site is known as Municipio S. Finds from the Iron Age were uncovered in *Gotovuša*. And, not to be forgotten: the monks in the 16th century *Trinity Monastery (Manastir Sv. Trojica)* in the centre of Pljevlja, who have one of the richest collections of icons, historical documents and books on the entire Balkan Peninsula. You will find nice and spacious rooms and the best cooking in the area at the hotel *Gold (9 rooms | Marka Miljanova | mobile 068 74 79 55 | booking on www.booking.com | Moderate)*.

TARA ★

(124–125 B–D 1–4) (*U–W 11–13*)

This is not only the longest river in the country, it is also the most beautiful: the Tara winds its way for 158 km/98 mi through the Montenegrin landscape, cutting through rocks and, shortly after Leveri, plunging 1,300 m/4,265 ft down a dozen cascades. The river has created the deepest canyon in Europe and – after the Grand Canyon – the second deepest worldwide; reason enough for the Unesco to declare the river a World Heritage Site in 1977. The Tara, which the Montenegrins have christened the "Tear of Europe", flows so slowly near the town of *Bistrica* that one can even wade through the water. This place has been nicknamed the "Devil's Lies" because the locals claim that it is possible to leap from one side to the other with a single jump.

The Montenegrins believe that everyone should journey down the Tara – in a kayak, boat or on an inflatable raft – at least once in a lifetime (see p. 104). The view from high up is also spectacular. In 1941, the bridge builder Lazar Janković spanned the ● ⚶ *Đurđevića Tara Bridge* 150 m/ 492 ft high above the river shortly after Đurđevića (25 km/15.5 mi east of Žabljak). Just one year later, he blew up the central arch in an attempt to prevent the advance of the German National Socialist troops. Switch off the car engine and enjoy a stroll over the bridge and back. You don't see views like this into the abyss every day! Near the bridge **INSIDER TIP** *Redrock-zipline (mobile 069 44 02 90 | www.red rockzipline.com | 10 euros) offers a crazy adventure*: hang on tight to the zipwire and fly up to 50 km/h/31 mph across the canyon. The small **INSIDER TIP** *Motel Tara MB (10 rooms | Đurđevića Tara bb | mobile 069 99 37 73 | www.mbturist.com | Moderate)* with a pleasant restaurant and lovely rooms is located by the bridge. If possible, you should book the ⚶ large room with a small balcony and panoramic views of the bridge and canyon.

ORTHODOX CHURCH

There are numerous orthodox medieval churches, monasteries and chapels all over the north of Montenegro; many of them are decorated with magnificent frescoes and icons. They are among the sacred sites of the orthodox faith, the exegesis of Christianity that was promoted after the division of the Roman Empire. In the Middle Ages the churches were places of sanctuary in the battle against the Turks. The Montenegrin Orthodox Church lost its independence when the country became part of Yugoslavia in 1918. In the socialist state religion was not desirable and the churches remained empty. In 1993, the Montenegrin Orthodox Church again split from its Serbian Orthodox brothers in Belgrade. Since then, the two religious communities have been in dispute with no resolution in sight. Today, three out of four Montenegrins describe themselves as orthodox Christians.

THE NORTH-EAST

Mountains over 2,000 m/6,562 ft high with their peaks capped by snow until well into summer, deep valleys, crystal-clear rivers and shimmering blue lakes: there is a new surprise around every corner in this area where four countries – Serbia, Albania, the Kosovo and Montenegro – come together.

Those in search of peace and quiet, away from the bustling tourist resorts on the Adriatic, will find it here in the fresh alpine air. And that at any time of the year – no matter whether it is on one of the numerous hiking trails through the Bjelasica Mountains, along the Mrtvica and Morača Canyons or skiing downhill from Mount Ćupović. Hidden away in the north-eastern highlands between Kolašin, Bijelo Polje and Berane is the Biogradska Gora National Park with one of the last primeval forests in Europe. And, in the centre is Biogradsko jezero, the enchanted glacial lake that gave the national park its name, where the mirrored reflection of the sky on the lake shimmers on its waters.

More than anywhere else in Montenegro, the traces of Turkish rule have remained alive in the Sandžak region: you will hear the Muezzins calling the faithful to pray from the minarets of centuries-old mosques.

BIJELO POLJE

(125 E3) *(ⅿ W12)* **This city (pop. 16,000) is just 20 km/12.4 mi from the Serbian**

Ski slopes and environmental protection: a Mecca for winter sports enthusiasts and an unspoiled national park

border. Its name means "white field" after the splendid mass of wild flowers that adorn Bijelo Polje every year in spring.

But the hilly landscape around the community on the banks of the Lim River is also completely white in winter: the skiing region in the Bjelasica Mountains is only a short distance away.

Founded in the 12th century, Bijelo Polje soon developed into a cultural and religious centre. It is situated on the banks of the Lim that flows northwards towards

Serbia. The city, which is surrounded by countless springs, became a bishop's seat in 1321 but came under Turkish control shortly thereafter. Today, thanks to its tourist infrastructure it makes an excellent starting point for exploring Montenegro's exciting north-eastern region.

SIGHTSEEING

SV. NIKOLA (ST NICHOLAS CHURCH)

The church on the bank of the Lim River has a library from the 14th century where

Still in a very good condition: the Đurđevi stupovi monastery near Berane

dozens of valuable manuscripts and early printed books are housed.

INSIDER TIP ▶ SV. PETAR (ST PETER'S CHURCH)

One of the most important Orthodox manuscripts (the Miroslav Gospel) was created in this church at the end of the 12th century. A copy of the document is on display in the nave of the church while – to the annoyance of the locals – the original is kept in the Serbian capital Belgrade. The whitewashed church tower was once used as a minaret: after the Turks conquered the city, they converted the church into a mosque and members of the Christian faith were not able to worship in it again until 1912.

FOOD & DRINK

There are restaurants and cafés in the centre of the small town. Most of them offer so-called "continental cuisine" with a lot of meat and not many vegetables. The prices are fairly reasonable wherever you eat.

RESTORAN KARAVAN ☆

The motel restaurant is in the suburbs, on the main road 10 km/6.2 mi north of the centre of Bijelo Polje, but the view of the Lim River from the spacious terrace is unique. Lamb and goat, oven-roast, are some of the specialities. *Mobile 068 13 75 61 | Budget–Moderate*

WHERE TO STAY

DOMINUS

It's hard to believe that here at the back of beyond there is such a well-appointed, cosy hotel with full amenities and very friendly staff. *Đorđija Stanića 31 | tel. 050 43 27 33 | www.hoteldominus.com | Budget*

Nedeljka Merdovića bb | tel. 050 48 47 95 | www.tobijelopolje.me

WHERE TO GO

The small towns in the area around Kolašin, such as *Rožaje* (125 F4) (*m̥ X13*) (pop. 9,000, 64 km/39.8 mi away) and *Andrijevica* (125 E4) (*m̥ W13*) (pop. 1,000, 50 km/31.1 mi to the east), have also developed into centres of tourism. You can ski here in winter and nature lovers and sports enthusiasts will also find plenty of activities to keep them busy in summer. The tourism office in Rožaje *(tel. 051 27 01 58)* provides information.

BERANE (125 E4) (*m̥ X13*)

It was once a sleepy backwater, but Berane (pop. 12,000, 36 km/22.4 mi south) flourished in Tito's Yugoslavia. The city was renamed Ivangrad after a heroic son of the city and war hero Ivan Milutinović; factories were built and the people had work. However, when Yugoslavia disintegrated, this prosperity disappeared along with the name. That didn't affect interest in the idyllic location – almost 700 m/2,297 ft high on the banks of the Lim River and surrounded by mountains. The gentle winds attract more and more paragliders here. Nearby is the well-preserved 13th-century monastery *Đurđevi stupovi*. You can spend the night at the reasonably priced hotel *Il Sole (28 rooms | Polimska 76 | mobile 067 46 33 33 | www.ilsolehotel.com | Moderate)*. In the *Il Sole* restaurant *(Budget)*, 100 m/328 ft from the banks of the Lim River, you can enjoy a delicious meal with the locals.

KOLAŠIN

(125 D4) (*m̥ W13*) **This is the most important winter sports town (pop. 3,000) in the north-east of Montenegro and lies at an altitude of 960 m/3,150 ft. It is also the country's water divide.**

While the Tara flows towards the Drina and then to the Black Sea by way of the Danube, the Morača's course is towards the Adriatic. Its proximity to the Bjelasica ski centre and Biogradska Gora National Park makes Kolašin a second ideal starting point for tours in the north-east.

FOOD & DRINK

INSIDER TIP ▶ **SAVARDAK**

The name says it all: *Savardak* are the pyramid-like highland huts and the

---

★ **Biogradska Gora Nacionalni Park**
Unwind in one of the world's oldest protected ecological areas surrounded by primeval forests and glacial lakes → **p. 88**

★ **Manastir Morača**
The magnificent frescoes in this important 13th century monastery bear witness to the influence of the Serbian Orthodox Church in the Middle Ages → **p. 89**

★ **Plav**
A delightful contrast near the border to Albania: mosques from the 18th century and an alpine lake between "enchanted" mountains that tower over 2,000 m/6,562 ft → **p. 89**

MARCO POLO HIGHLIGHTS

restaurant (on the way out of town towards the Bjelasica ski centre) is housed in one of them. The restaurant's speciality is hearty grilled food. You should definitely try the cheesy Montenegrin polenta *kačamak* or the wheat stew *cicvara*! *Biocinovići | mobile 069 05 12 64 | Budget*

LEISURE & SPORTS

Skiing in the daytime and at night? That's no problem in the winter sports centre *Bjelasica* at 1,200 m/3,937 ft to 1,450 m/4,757 ft. You pay about 20 euros for a ski pass. In summer you can also enjoy plenty of sports around Kolašin and in the national park: hiking, rafting, tubing, even jeep safaris. The *Tourist Agency Sport Turist (Junaka Mojkovačke Bitke | mobile 068 00 30 56 | www.sport turist.me)* has a wide range of offers for all these activities. The young, English-speaking staff are also professional and friendly.

WHERE TO STAY

BIANCA RESORT & SPA
The Bianca is a contemporary wood and stone construction with a gigantic swimming pool, spa and wellness complex set in the heart of the mountains. The elegant establishment is one of the best hotels in the country. *115 rooms | Mirka Vešovića | tel. 020 86 30 00 | www.bianca resort.com | Moderate–Expensive*

ČILE
In the rustic guesthouse you will get a friendly welcome. There is also good local food. *9 rooms | Dunje Djokić | tel. 020 86 50 39 | www.hotelcile.me | Budget–Moderate*

INSIDER TIP ▸ VILA JELKA ⊚
The "Fir Villa" is more than just a charming family pension. They also offer a winning combination: spend the night in wooden huts and then enjoy a whole-food meal including fish and meat from the region. The leisure activities include rafting, hiking and Jeep tours. But beware: in the colder season the conditions in the region are icy and cold. And the "villa" is not really a villa but more a camp site. *8 rooms | tel. 020 86 01 50 | www.jelka.me | Budget–Moderate*

INFORMATION

Mirka Vešovića | tel. 020 86 42 54

WHERE TO GO

BIOGRADSKA GORA NACIONALNI PARK ★ (125 D–E 3–4) (∅ W12–13)
One of the last primeval forests in Europe is within the nature reserve (15 km/9.3 mi north-east) that was declared a national park in 1952. Preserving so much unspoiled nature in such a small area is not least thanks to Prince Nikola I. As early as in 1878, only six years after Yellowstone National Park was established in the USA, he proclaimed Biogradska Gora an environmentally protected area. Today, the park has about 2,000 types of plants and over 200 bird species. The lakes here, which are known

LOW BUDGET

At the restaurant INSIDER TIP ▸ *Konoba (Trg Vukmana Kruščića | mobile 069 60 91 44)* in Kolašin, in a small, rustic wooden hut you eat simple, traditional dishes for very reasonable prices. That makes it at least double the fun!

In the national park around Lake Biogrdsko not only the butterflies feel good!

as "eyes of the mountain" (gorske oči) are particularly interesting. The loveliest is *Lake Biogradsko (Biogradsko jezero)*. *Eco-Tours (Dunje Đokić | Kolašin | mobile 067 25 90 20 | www.eco-tours.co.me)* have a wide variety of activities on offer. Do you want to hike, to cycle or to ride horses in the national park? It's up to you.

MANASTIR MORAČA ★
(125 D4) (*Ω V13*)

Morača Monastery, built in 1252, is one of the most important Serbian Orthodox monasteries. It lies approx. 30 km/18.6 mi south-west of Kolašin, just after the confluence of the Mrtvica and Morača Rivers. The frescoes that were painted in the 16th and 17th centuries, after the church had been plundered by the Turks, will stick in your memory. *Daily 8am–6pm*

PLAV ★ (125 E5) (*Ω X14*)

Fascinating: Plav (pop. 2,000), 63 km/ 39.2 mi to the south-east, has two mosques from the 18th century. The *Vezirova Mosque* dates from 1741 and the *Redžepagića Mosque* was built three decades later. The Kula Redžepagića defensive tower of the former ruling family is just up the hill from the mosque. The mountain lake *Plavsko jezero* is tucked away in the dense forests close to the town. It lies at the foot of Mount Prokletije (2,700 m/8,858 ft), which is known among locals as the "cursed mountain" because of its steep, bare walls.

Plav is an excellent starting point for cross-border trekking tours in Montenegro, Albania and the Kosovo. The transnational **INSIDER TIP** *"Peaks of the Balkans Trail' (www.peaksofthebalkans. com)* is a demanding hike into the isolated Prokletije region. The tour is 192 km/119 mi long and takes around ten days accompanied by experienced mountain guides. It passes through spectacular landscapes, barren mountain massifs, secluded lakes, waterfalls, alpine pastures full of flowers and picturesque villages. Mountaineering experience is essential.

DISCOVERY TOURS

1

MONTENEGRO
AT A GLANCE

START: ❶ Herceg Novi
END: ❶ Herceg Novi

Distance:
🚗 approx. 580 km/360 mi

3 days
Driving time
(without stops)
13 hours

COSTS: approx. 350 euros/2 persons (petrol, food and drink, overnight stay, admissions, activities)

WHAT TO PACK: warm clothing, swimming gear

IMPORTANT TIP: Phone ahead and book an appointment with the runner-up world champion hairdresser, Style by Eky, in ❿ Bijelo Polje.

Explore the coastline, rocky cliffs and ancient culture in no time – few other small countries have so much to offer at one go. The places of worship of four religions

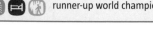

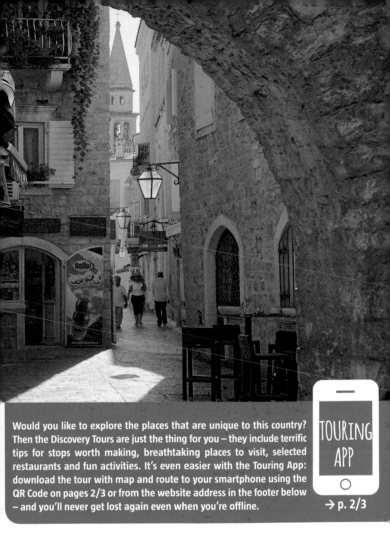

Would you like to explore the places that are unique to this country? Then the Discovery Tours are just the thing for you – they include terrific tips for stops worth making, breathtaking places to visit, selected restaurants and fun activities. It's even easier with the Touring App: download the tour with map and route to your smartphone using the QR Code on pages 2/3 or from the website address in the footer below – and you'll never get lost again even when you're offline.

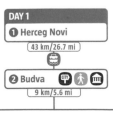

TOURING APP

→ p. 2/3

and the testimony of an eventful history reveal Montenegro's past and present. Most of all, however, you will discover the country's wild beauty and its never-ending, breathtaking panoramic views.

From ❶ **Herceg Novi** → p. 34 **drive on the E 65 in the direction of Kotor as far as Kamenari. Take the ferry to Lepetane. On the E 80, after Tivat, continue uphill** and ahead of you lies ❷ **Budva** → p. 53. Park the car before the **old town**, stroll through the narrow streets and travel back in time in the **city museum** and the days of the

DAY 1

❶ Herceg Novi

43 km/26.7 mi

❷ Budva

9 km/5.6 mi

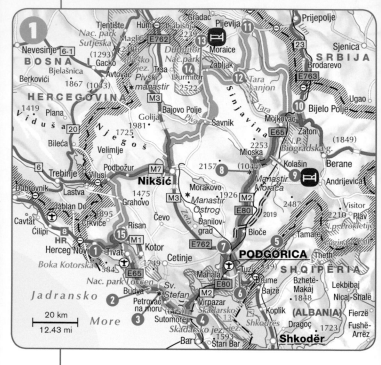

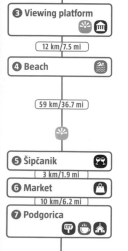

3 Viewing platform 🏞️ 🏛️

⎯⎯⎯ 12 km/7.5 mi ⎯⎯⎯

4 Beach 🏊

⎯⎯⎯ 59 km/36.7 mi ⎯⎯⎯

🏞️

5 Šipčanik 🍷

⎯⎯⎯ 3 km/1.9 mi ⎯⎯⎯

6 Market 🛍️

⎯⎯⎯ 10 km/6.2 mi ⎯⎯⎯

7 Podgorica 🛍️ ☕ 🏠

Roman Empire. **On the E 80 heading for Petrovac na Moru**, a **3** viewing platform → p. 57 is signposted, where you can see the former fishing village of **Sv. Stefan** in all its glory. **Immediately after Petrovac, turn right on a small road to Buljarica** → p. 59. Go for a swim in the Adriatic on the long, usually pleasantly empty **4** beach.

The E 80 leads to the Sozina Tunnel in the direction of Podgorica. On the other side of the mountains, Lake Skadar glimmers in the sunshine, and you cross the plain of Ćemovsko polje where vines are cultivated. **Shortly before Podgorica head for the E 762, and follow the signs to the wine cellar at **5** Šipčanik → p. 72** and for the wine tasting 30 m/98.4 ft below ground. The short journey to the next stop at **Tuzi** is signposted. Enjoy bargaining at Montenegro's largest **6** market → p. 30. **Back on the E 762 head for **7** Podgorica → p. 69.** In **Njegoševa street** you can experience the flair of the capital city. Young people enjoy meeting here, while bars and boutiques dominate the street scene. In the popular **Kafić Berlin** → p. 18 try the fashionable drink *dojčkafa*, a "German coffee". Afterwards, look inside Montenegro's largest orthodox church, the **Cathedral of the Resurrection of Christ**.

After Podgorica, continue your journey on the E 80. Here is the start of Moračas Canyon, and the emerald green river glimmers far below. Visit the centuries-old frescoes and enjoy the peace in the orthodox ⑧ **Morača Monastery** → p. 89, before **continuing on the E 80 to Kolašin** → p. 87. Here, after a relaxing Hawaiian or Thai massage you can stay overnight at the ⑨ **Bianca Resort & Spa**.

On the winding E 80 to ⑩ **Bijelo Polje** → p. 84, Bjelasica Mountains and its high peaks accompany the journey. Mosques and minarets dominate the cityscape, although you also discover medieval orthodox churches. How about a special souvenir? At INSIDER TIP **Style by Eky** *(Ul. Đorđa Stanića bb | mobile. 069 23 31 66)*, you can have a new haircut by the world's second most renowned Figaro: Eky-Eldin Krivošić was runner-up in the 2016 World Hairdressing Championship.

On the R 10 you arrive in Pljevlja → p. 82 with the impressive ⑪ **Hussein Pasha Mosque**. **The R 4 mountain route has plenty of hairpin bends, after Odžak and Vilići**, a viewing platform overlooks ⑫ **Đurđevića Tara Bridge** → p. 83. A different outlook awaits you on the bridge: the Tara River meanders below, while high above are the Durmitor Mountain peaks. **Redrockzipline** sends you on an adventurous flight along the bridge. **The R 5 continues through unspoiled countryside to Durmitor National Park.** In **Žabljak** → p. 79 at the rustic ⑬ **Autocamp Razvršje** treat yourself to Mama's local cuisine and stay overnight in cosy farmers' huts.

Before you continue your journey, catch a glimpse of nearby ⑭ **Crno jezero** → p. 81, Durmitor's most scenic lake. **Back on the winding R 5, via Šavnik, drive into the valley and on the E 762 head for Nikšić. First, stay on the E 762 bypass, and then onto the M 6 in the direction of Bosnia-Herzegovina. Shortly before the border, near Vilusi, turn left onto the R 11 towards Herceg Novi and Risan** → p. 44, where you can see the Roman mosaics in the ⑮ **open-air museum**. **The E 80**

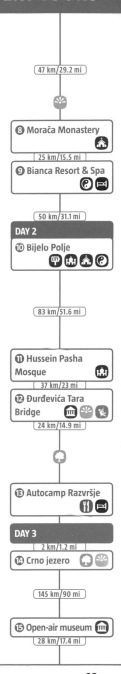

heads back to **1** **Herceg Novi**. Park outside the centre and walk through the city of 1,000 steps to the harbour. Take the Barkarioli on a night-time boat excursion to **Modra Špilja** → p. 47 – for INSIDER TIP a moonlit swim in the blue grotto.

2 FROM THE COAST TO THE ROCKY CLIFFS AND BACK

START: **1** Tivat **END:** **1** Tivat	**2 days** Driving time (without stops) 7.5 hours
Distance: approx. 230 km/143 mi	

COSTS: approx. 300 euros/2 persons (petrol, food and drink, overnight stay, admissions, activities, sun loungers)
WHAT TO PACK: swimming gear, water, sun screen

On the old route with hairpin bends leading to the centre of the country, you drive uphill into the rugged mountain terrain near Kotor and the historic capital of Cetinje. Then, make the descent again – to swim in the deep blue bays between Budva and Tivat. On the coast, you can look forward to exceptional water quality and beach cocktail bars.

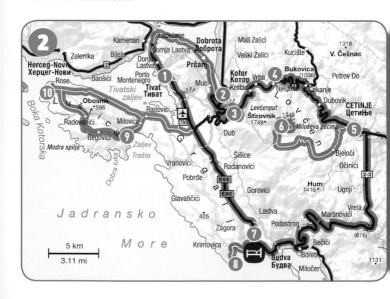

The tour begins in ❶ **Tivat** → **p. 45** with an unusual discovery: feel the tight space in the ex-submarine of the Yugoslavian navy in front of the **Museum Arsenal**. **On the E 80 drive onwards to Lepetane and via Prčanj to ❷ Kotor → p. 39.** You can watch the big cruise ships from the promenade, as they navigate through the fjord. Walk through the medieval **old town** to St Tryphon's Cathedral.

When you leave Kotor at the southern end of the city, you reach a crossroads after about 4 km/2.5 mi where you turn left onto the R 1 and uphill in the direction of Cetinje. Here is the start of the ❸ **Ladder of Cattaro** — until the end of the 19th century it was the only access route to the middle of the country. It winds its way uphill and offers breathtaking views of the Bay of Kotor, the most impressive vista is **shortly before the village of Krstač**. Soon you arrive at **Njeguši → p. 69**, which is not only the birthplace of the poet Prince Njegoš, but is also famous for smoked ham and hard cheese. Try at ❹ **Kod Pera Na Bukovicu. After Njeguši the R 1 continues uphill** and the sparse mountain landscape is revealed in all its glory. In the museums of ❺ **Cetinje → p. 65** you can discover the country's history and the magnificent old **embassy buildings**. On the gigantic relief map in the museum in **Biljarda** you can even see Montenegro from a bird's eye perspective.

A detour continues on the well-marked route to Lovćen National Park to the large ❻ Njegoš Mausoleum → p. 68. From the nearby viewing platform, on clear days the view reaches as far as the mountains of Albania. **Back in Cetinje you continue on the M 2–3 in the direction of Budva**. On the other side of the mountain, quite unexpectedly there is a far-reaching vista of the Adriatic. **Drive onwards on the E 80 towards Tivat past Budva. After the mountain and about 3 km/1.9 mi further on, take the turning to ❼ Jaz → p. 54.** At the eastern end of the beach – a length of 1,200 m/3,937 ft – is the **Hotel Poseidon** *(60 rooms | mobile 069 41 12 40 | www.poseidon-jaz. com | Budget–Moderate)*. Enjoy a swim and the evening sunset and stay overnight here.

Chill out in Kotor old town

DAY 1

❶ Tivat 🏛

17 km/10.6 mi

❷ Kotor 🌿 🍽 🏛 🏠

11 km/6.8 mi

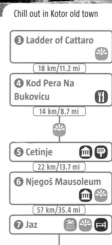

❸ Ladder of Cattaro 🌿

18 km/11.2 mi

❹ Kod Pera Na Bukovicu 🍽

14 km/8.7 mi

🌿

❺ Cetinje 🏛 🍽

22 km/13.7 mi

❻ Njegoš Mausoleum 🏛 🌿

57 km/35.4 mi

❼ Jaz 🌊 🌿 🏖

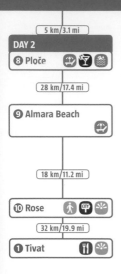

5 km/3.1 mi	
DAY 2	
❽ Ploče	🚗 🍸 🏊
28 km/17.4 mi	
❾ Almara Beach	🚗
18 km/11.2 mi	
❿ Rose	🚶 🏙 ☀
32 km/19.9 mi	
❶ Tivat	🍴 ☀

The country road continues past the Bay of Trsteno and onwards to the trendy beach ❽ **Ploče** with pools, cocktail bars, rock and electronic music. For the young people here, swimming is not so important, even if the deep blue sea beckons. **From the E 80 in the direction of Tivat, turn off before the airport and head for the country road to Radovići and the sophisticated** ❾ **Almara Beach** → **p. 46** to relax beneath a sun canopy.

Now you can explore Luština Peninsula. **The country road heads back to Radovići, and shortly before the coast turn left to Krašići. Here, you leave the coastal road and drive through olive groves and deserted villages to Klinci.** Take a stroll through the idyllic artist village ❿ **Rose** → **p. 47**, and enjoy the view over the Bay of Kotor. **On the coastal road head for Krašići. After the village follow the signs to the airport and the tour now heads back to** ❶ **Tivat** and the marina of **Porto Montenegro**. In the Lebanese restaurant **Byblos** enjoy oriental specialities and the view of the luxury yachts.

❸ HIGH-FLYERS IN HIKING BOOTS

START: ❶ Kolašin		2 days
END: ❶ Kolašin		Hiking
Trail:	medium	(without stops)
🕐 39 km/24.2 mi .ıl	Altitude: 1,000 m/3,281 ft	15 hours

COSTS: approx. 250 euros/2 persons (food and drink, overnight stay, hiking guide, admissions, boat hire, return transfer)
WHAT TO PACK: helmet, hiking boots, warm clothing (temperature in summer: 12–15 °C (54–59 °F), rain wear, picnic, water, sunglasses

IMPORTANT TIPS: Confirm the details in advance with the tour operator **Eco-Tours** *(Dunje Đokić | Kolašin | mobile 067 25 90 20 | www.eco-tours.co.me)*: guide, overnight stay before and after the hike and on the way *(only possible in May–Nov)*, collection by private car or hired car from Lake Biogradsko *(approx. 20 km/ 12.5 mi)*. Don't set off without a guide! Although all the paths are well marked, the weather can suddenly change (danger of lightning strikes!). Always follow the advice of your guide and do not leave the marked paths! Your baggage should not be too heavy.

Hiking in Biogradska Gora National Park you can almost reach the sky!

The primeval forest in Biogradska Gora National Park is a paradise for hikers. Climb the high mountains, visit old chapels and mountain huts, trek along wolf trails and enjoy the peace and quiet at the idyllic Lake Biogradsko.

In ❶ **Kolašin** → p. 87 from your accommodation **Bije-li Potok** walk **along the road in the direction of Dulov-ine as far as the outskirts of town**. A signpost marks the way to the **Botanical Garden** that offers you a first glimpse of the mountain wildflowers. **A gravel road continues in the direction of Izlasci into the mountains, partly along a stream and through increasingly dense forest. Past Izlas-ci you reach ❷ Ćirilovac Monastery**. In the main church, light a candle according to the orthodox custom, and make a wish. Then, it's time for a refreshing picnic. **On forest footpaths continue hiking uphill towards Mount ❸ Ključ** (1,973 m/6,473 ft). In summer, you cross fragrant meadows and can pick forest berries, and in late autumn you can hear the distant howl of the wolf. The region is renowned for the wolves and brown bears that live off the beaten tracks. Walk to the summit and the **chapel**. Here, you have a pan-oramic view of the mountains in north-east Montenegro.

DAY 1

❶ Kolašin

11 km/6.8 mi

❷ Ćirilovac Monastery

4 km/2.5 mi

❸ Ključ

5 km/3.1 mi

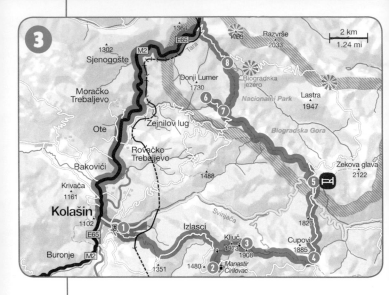

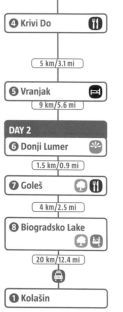

④ Krivi Do 🍴

5 km/3.1 mi

⑤ Vranjak 🛏

9 km/5.6 mi

DAY 2

⑥ Donji Lumer 🌐

1.5 km/0.9 mi

⑦ Goleš 🌳🍴

4 km/2.5 mi

⑧ Biogradsko Lake 🌳🛏

20 km/12.4 mi

🚌

① Kolašin

The higher you climb on the footpath, the more frequently you encounter the *katuni*, or mountain huts, some of which are still in use. When you reach the summer pasture, or Katun 🌐 **④ Krivi Do**, you have earned a break. Here, you should try the home-produced cheeses *lisnati sir* and *kajmak*. It's best to drink the schnapps *rakija* slowly and with a glass of water so that the spirits don't burn the throat. Then, continue climbing even higher to 1,750 m/5,741 ft to Katun **⑤ Vranjak**, and stay overnight in a wooden hut.

Next morning, make the **descent in the direction of the lake. From the summit ⑥ Donji Lumer** you have an amazing view of Biogradsko jezero, Lake Biograd. At the Katun 🌐 **⑦ Goleš** at an altitude of 1,600 m/5,249 ft, along with sheep, goats, barking dogs and bird song you are greeted by INSIDER TIP exceptional cuisine made with regional ingredients: lamb, boiled in milk or roasted in hot ashes, corn hash, thick yogurt and freshly baked bread that is still warm. After the meal, you can rent a boat in the Katun and make the descent **through the primeval forest to ⑧ Lake Biogradsko → p. 89**. Having reached the end of your hiking tour, you deserve a rest, while you paddle gently across the water. A driver will collect you for the journey – as arranged in advance with Eco Tours – back to **① Kolašin**.

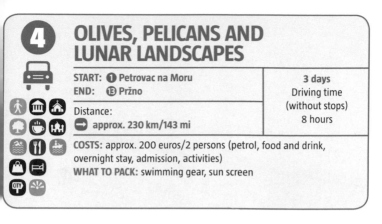

4 OLIVES, PELICANS AND LUNAR LANDSCAPES

START: ❶ Petrovac na Moru **END:** ⓭ Pržno	3 days Driving time (without stops) 8 hours
Distance: ➡ approx. 230 km/143 mi	

COSTS: approx. 200 euros/2 persons (petrol, food and drink, overnight stay, admission, activities)
WHAT TO PACK: swimming gear, sun screen

There is plenty to discover between the Adriatic and Lake Skadar: ancient olive trees and organic olive oil, solitary mountain routes and deserted moon landscapes, pelicans and cormorants, churches, mosques and a remote convent are only a few highlights on this tour.

In ❶ **Petrovac na Moru → p. 57** your day starts off with a swim, and a walk through the fragrant pine forest to the beach at **Lučice. Then, head onto the E 80 for** ❷ **Bar → p. 50**. Enjoy the shopping experience at the **farmers' market**. Walk to the **harbour**, and watch the large ferries and container ships. In ❸ **Stari Bar → p. 52** stroll through the centuries-old ruins and surrender to the temptation of oriental delicacies from the Turkish **Patisserie Karađuzović**. A mocha goes perfectly with a sweet Baklava.

On the E 851 in the direction of Ulcinj you will notice an ❹ **olive tree → p. 52** which is among the oldest in the world. **The tree stands before the village of Tomba, and the route is marked.** The 2,200 year old tree is an amazing sight. In ❺ **Ulcinj → p. 61** you will meet your hostess for the night at **Vila Tamara. Close to your accommodation, near Hotel Albatros**, the **cliff-side beaches** are hidden away in dense pine forests. After a quick swim, **walk along a pedestrian footpath along the city beach into the old town**. On the terrace of the hotel **Kulla e Balshajve** enjoy the excellent fish dishes and the view over Ulcinj. Time to find a souvenir? The region's best silversmiths are in **Ulica zlatara**. A visit is equally worthwhile at **Olive Ponte → p. 19**.

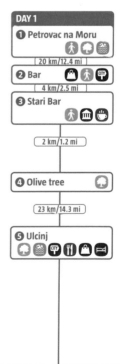

DAY 1

❶ Petrovac na Moru

20 km/12.4 mi

❷ Bar

4 km/2.5 mi

❸ Stari Bar

2 km/1.2 mi

❹ Olive tree

23 km/14.3 mi

❺ Ulcinj

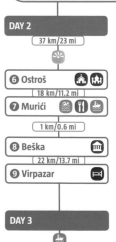

DAY 2

| 37 km/23 mi |

6 Ostroš 🏠 🏛️

| 18 km/11.2 mi |

7 Murići 🏖️ 🍴 🛏️

| 1 km/0.6 mi |

8 Beška 🏛️

| 22 km/13.7 mi |

9 Virpazar 🚗

DAY 3

Shortly after Krute, turn left off the E 851 and onto the R 16 in the direction of Virpazar. The impressive summits of Mount Rumija accompany the journey and soon Lake Skadar glimmers on the right. You pass small villages like **6 Ostroš** where Catholic churches stand alongside mosques. Drive as far as **7 Murići → p. 74. The lower part of the village of Donji Murići is situated right by the lake**. After a swim, enjoy fresh fish at the Restaurant **Izletište Murići** *(mobile 069 68 82 88 | Budget)*. Here, you can book a boat excursion to visit the monastery on the island of **8 Beška → p. 73. Continue by car to 9 Virpazar → p. 74**, where you can stay overnight in the **Guesthouse Vukasevic**. First, walk to the **visitors' centre** to book a boat excursion for the next day to Rijeka Crnojevića.

Early risers are rewarded with one of the most fabulous excursions that Lake Skadar has to offer: the two-hour return boat trip to Rijeka Crnojevića starts at 6am in the morning. You glide among water lilies to the river of the same name that meanders through the countryside like a fjord. On the way, you can see pelicans and cormorants, storks and falcons. Back in the car enjoy the unforgettable view from high above of the meandering watercourse, **when you drive on the R 16 to Rijeka Crnojevića. Shortly before the village follow the signposted country road to Gornji Ceklin** to the ⑩ **Farm Vukmirović.** Watch as the beekeeper spins the honey and enjoy a light snack. **The M 2–3 heads towards the coast. In Obzovica, leave the motorway for the country road in the direction of Utrg and Brčeli and head for the M 2 in the direction of Petrovac.** The barren mountains in this region are reminiscent of a lunar landscape. Your breath is taken away at the summit when the riviera of Budva stretches out in front of you.

On the hairpin bends make the descent and travel along the E 80 to ⑪ **Sv. Stefan → p. 56.** Enjoy a meal in the Restaurant **Olive**, and admire the view of the rocky and beautiful island. Round off the tour with a walk at the nearby beautiful natural bays of ⑫ **Miločer → p. 57** and ⑬ **Pržno → p. 56.**

31 km/19.3 mi

⑩ Farm Vukmirović

61 km/37.9 mi

⑪ Sv. Stefan

1 km/0.6 mi

⑫ Miločer

0.5 km/0.3 mi

⑬ Pržno

The wildlife paradise of Lake Skadar is best discovered by boat

SPORTS & ACTIVITIES

Sport is a form of punishment? No way! In Montenegro, everything is fun from fishing to windsurfing.

It is possible to ski in some mountain valleys until July. On the other hand, you can already explore the north of the country on snow-free trails in April. The infrastructure in the Bjelasica, Prokletije, Durmitor and Lovćen mountain regions, as well as around Lake Skadar, nowadays has been greatly improved with alpine huts, camping sites and sports clubs.

On the Adriatic coast you relax outside in the balmy spring air from April and diving is also not a problem – if you have a wetsuit in your luggage. The Adriatic has an average temperature of over 20 °C/68 °F until well into October providing ideal conditions for water sports such as snorkelling, swimming and sailing.

ANGLING

Dozens of rivers and hundreds of streams, countless lakes and not least the Adriatic Sea: Montenegro offers plenty of freshwater fishing grounds. An excellent tour company among the numerous fishing tour offers is *Kingfisher (mobile 067 01 90 95 | www.skadarlakeboatcruise.com)* in Virpazar on Lake Skadar. There is also a wide choice on the Adriatic coast. The Crno jezero near Žabljak and the Morača and Lim Rivers in the highlands are known for being especially rich in fish.

Sailing, skiing, hiking and rafting – there is an astonishing range of activities in this small country

DIVING

Pleasant water temperatures and interesting dive sites such as coral reefs, sunken ships and underwater caves make the Montenegrin Adriatic ideal for divers. The water along the coast is around 35 m/114.8 ft deep and the summer temperatures are between 21–25 °C/70–77 °F. The dive certificates issued by the established international organisations are recognised, however, it is only possible to dive with Monte-negrin companies. The international database *www.dive-centers.net* offers a good overview of the local enterprises – enter 'Montenegro' in the search field on the homepage.

MOUNTAINEERING & MOUNTAIN BIKING

An increasing number of visitors are leaving the beaches and getting out their hiking boots and bicycles to explore new territory far away from the coast.

A nationwide network of cycle and hiking paths of around 6,000 km/3,728 mi has been established within the framework of the Wilderness Hiking & Biking project in an effort to integrate the hinterland into the country's tourist activities. Almost all of the trails lead into the fascinating landscape of the north – where there are over 150 mountains that are more than 2,000 m/6,562 ft high. Most of the hikes are well marked with signposts.

Cyclists can choose between six national trails, ranging from easy-going to demanding, in addition to other local routes. Renting a bike can be difficult, especially if operators do not have enough bikes on hand. Ask at the local tourist office for more information. But be cautious and remember that your safety should always come first in the wild north of the country (see p. 136). It is recommended to take a guide who knows the area. The *mountain rescue service (Gorska sluzba spasavanja Crne Gore | www.gss-cg.me/english)* under tel. 040 25 60 84 or the police under tel. 122 can help in case of an emergency.

(see p. 136)

PARAGLIDING & KITESURFING

Along the coast Budva and Ada Bojana are popular spots for paragliders and kitesurfers. Strong winds, long beaches – ideal conditions to get airborne. But this is also possible on other beaches between Tivat and Ulcinj. *Paragliding Montenegro (www.paraglidingmontenegro.com | mobile 069 0 22 3 52)* offers information for paragliders. In the north, Berane is developing as a centre for the sport.

RAFTING

A rafting tour on the Tara River is one of the highlights of any holiday in Montenegro. The river carves its way for more than 100 km/62 mi through the highlands in the north-west – and provides lots of thrills and spills for the rafters. Tackling the frothing waves in the deep canyon is an unforgettable experience. Tour operators in Kolašin and Žabljak organise tours not only on the

Wet fun for the adventurous: rafting in the Tara Canyon

Tara River but also on the Piva River that joins the Tara at the border with Bosnia-Herzegovina. There are tours of various lengths and a long list of operators. Two operators from Kolašin provide offers throughout the north of the country and have exceptionally well-trained guides: *Explorer (Mojkovačka | mobile 067 26 3138 | www.explorer.co.me) and Eco-Tours (Dunje Đokić | mobile 067 25 90 20 | www.eco-tours.co.me)*.

SAILING

There are some well equipped marinas between Herceg Novi and Bar for Adriatic yachtsmen. The Porto Montenegro *(www.portomontenegro.com)* operation in Tivat aims to outdo Monaco and Saint Tropez. The countless regattas – mainly for small and medium-mast boats – show just how important this sport is in Montenegro. You can charter yachts and motor boats in any of the larger towns on the coast. Podgorica is also the headquarter of the *Montenegro Charter Company (Bulevar Sv. Petra Cetinjskog 92 | mobile 067 20 16 55 | www.montenegro charter.com)*.

SKIING

Thanks to the exceptional infrastructure and empty slopes for reasonable prices (day pass 15–20 euros) as well as reasonably for renting skiing equipment (approx. 15 euros per day), Montenegro is a popular destination for winter sports fans.The continental climate in the north guarantees freezing winters with plenty of snow in the Montenegrin mountains. The season lasts from December to April. Durmitor near Žabljak and Bjelasica near Kolašin are the best known of Montenegro's numerous skiing regions with slopes up to 2,000 m/6,562 ft.

TENNIS

Novak Đoković is for Montenegro what Andy Murray is for the United Kingdom. Although the international tennis star is Serbian, his family comes from the country of the black mountains – this is why he is celebrated here as "our Novak". The Canadian-born Milos Raonic, from Podgorica, who ranked among the top players in the world for years, is also regarded as "one of us". The Montenegrins' love of tennis makes the tennis association *Teniski Savez Crne Gore (www.mta.co.me)* popular. This also benefits tourists, as many coastal resorts now have tennis courts, for example, in Herceg Novi, Tivat, Budva, Bar or Ada Bojana. Tennis courts are also found inland, e.g., in Podgorica, Berane or Nikšić. You will find the addresses at local tourist offices, registration is necessary.

WELLNESS

Wellness? A decade ago it was unknown, but now wellness offers are everywhere. The first offers were by large luxury hotels in the centre of the country, which opened spas, e.g. in Kolašin, as well as along the coast in Bečići or Budva. You can generally use the services as a day guest, a day pass costs between 15 and 30 euros.

WINDSURFING

Do you love surfing? Then, head for Ulcinj – big waves and strong winds are guaranteed here! Beginners, on the other hand, should enjoy the protected waters of the Bay of Kotor. It is also fun to try the fresh-water variety: people have recently started windsurfing on Lake Skadar once again.

TRAVEL WITH KIDS

There is a Montenegrin saying that children are the happiness of the world. They take an active part in family life and are often allowed to stay up very late. And the offspring of foreign guests are also usually free to do as they please. Ask for *igraonica* (pronounced 'igraonizza'), plagrounds with a range of activities and toys for inside and outside. Water slides and pedal boats can be found at almost every beach. For the really adventurous there are diving courses especially for children.

Ask for discounts for children when booking a hotel. Even though children's portions are not listed on the menu, restaurants are usually happy to oblige if requested. Take care on the roads and paths because they frequently lack pavements.

BAY OF KOTOR

The international children's carnival is held in June in Herceg Novi (126 C5) (*ₐ H5*) and the colourful splendour of the summer carnival in Kotor (127 E–F 4–5) (*ₐ K5*) in August will really delight the little ones. A unique sight is the *Fašinada* in July, a procession on the water when rowing boats with torches make their way from Perast (127 D–E4) (*ₐ J4*) to the island of Gospa od Škrpjela. For festival dates go to *www.montenegro.travel*.

CETINJE, PODGORICA & LAKE SKADAR

In Biljarda in Cetinje (128 C3–4) (*ₐ L–M4*) there is a new way for you to make the family's travel route more entertaining. The giant INSIDER TIP *relief map (admission Biljarda adults 3.50 euros, children 1 euro, relief map 1 euro extra)* in the southern part of the museum courtyard shows the whole of Montenegro at a glance.

A thrilling outdoor experience for kids and parents is a visit to the *Avanturistički park Lovćen* (128 B4) (*ₐ L5*) *(Ivanova Korita | 15 April–May, 15 Sept–Oct Sat, Sun 12pm–6pm, June–15 Sept daily 10am–6pm, admission adults 18 euros, children 8–13 years 12 euros, 5–8 years 8 euros | www.avanturistickipark.com)*, an adventure park covering 5 acres in the Lovćen Mountains. Amidst unspoiled nature you can climb, slide, crawl and jump over obstacles.

On the outskirts of Podgorica is the *Konjički klub Poni* (124 C5) (*ₐ O2*)

Horseback riding on the beach, petting animals on a farm, diving in the Adriatic – Montenegro offers a great deal to young visitors

(Vranići | mobile 068 719404 | www. konjickiklubpony.yolasite.com), a pony riding club with a mini-zoo.

THE ADRIATIC

A 1.85 acres large *Aquapark (day pass adults 15, children 10 euros)* is part of the *Mediteran (230 rooms | tel. 033 424382 | www.mediteran.me | Expensive) hotel complex in Bečići* (128 C5) *(*🗺️ *M6)*. There are two swimming pools especially for children.

Holidaymakers who go to the Adriatic with their offspring in November – it is often still possible to swim then – can visit the *Susreti pod starom maslinom* exhibition near Bar (130 A–B 4–5) *(*🗺️ *P7)*. Children display their works on the theme of 'Olive, Peace, Friendship' under the oldest olive tree in the country. Children can learn to ride on the Grand Beach in Ulcinj (131 D6) *(*🗺️ *R8)*. Riding lessons can be booked locally at the hotels that are members of the *Ulcinjska rivijera* association.

THE NORTH-EAST

The INSIDER TIP *botanical garden* (125 D4) *(*🗺️ *W13) (Botanička Bašta | daily 9am–6pm | admission adults 3 euros, children 2 euros)* in Dulovina near the town of Kolašin has a collection of the region's rare plants. The life's work of the so-called herb king of Montenegro, Daniel Vincek, is a small paradise that is not only fascinating for children but equally informative for adults.

THE NORTH-WEST

The pristine Durmitor still has farms (124–125 B–D 2–3) *(*🗺️ *U–W 11–12)* where goat and sheep milk cheese is made by hand from the milk of free-range animals. To get there just ask locally where you can find a *katun*. The proverbially hospitable Montenegrins will let the children willingly play with their animals and show them how they make cheese.

FESTIVALS & EVENTS

In Montenegro, most official public holidays are followed by another holiday day. The details are provided in the information box on p. 109. Exact details of events are often announced at short notice. If no dates are provided on this page, please ask the locals or take a look on the website of the tourist organisation *www.montenegro.travel*.

FESTIVALS & EVENTS

FEBRUARY
Mimosa Festival in Herceg Novi. The first mimosa blossoms are greeted with fanfare on the waterfront promenade.
During the carnival period there are masked balls and colourful processions in many places along the coast, among them the *Carnival in Kotor*.

APRIL
Palm Sunday (Vrbica) is a special day for children in the Orthodox Church. People make wreathes out of palm fronds for a grand procession, then the priest arrives ringing his little bell and blesses the festival procession with lots of incense.
The theatre festival *HAPS* is held in the second half of the month in Herceg Novi.

On 30 April the International Jazz Day is celebrated in ten large towns including Podgorica, Budva and Kotor: *Jazz at Noon* is fun!

MAY
Free climbers shin up the steep cliffs in Kotor and Nikšić in their attempts to win the *Montenegro Cup*.
The *Night of the Museums* is celebrated throughout the country on 19 May
Tito's Birthday is still celebrated on 25 May in Tivat with flags and revolutionary songs.

JULY
Fashion Week in Kotor shows Dior and Gucci along with creations by local Montenegrin designers.
INSIDER TIP *Festival of Male Choirs* in Perast. The *klape* have no more than eight members and perform their repertoire a capella.
Bridge Diving in Mojkovac: the brave jump into the river from the Tara Bridge. The most impressive jumps are awarded.
The INSIDER TIP *Sea Dance Festival (www.seadancefestival.me)* is an absolute insider tip amoung the European music events. Partygoers dance to rock

Montenegrins love to celebrate festivals: the new season starts with the first spring festival just after Christmas

and electro sounds on the Jaz Beach near Budva.

During the INSIDER**TIP** *Classical Music Festival* musicians from around the world bring the sound of music to Herceg Novi.

AUGUST

Films from the region and from all over the world are shown at the *Herceg Novi Film Festival (www.filmfesti val.me)* held at the beginning of the month in the fortress Kanli kula in Herceg Novi. Although not all of the films are shown with English subtitles, the screenings in the open air are a great experience.

Expert collectors show everything that grows in the area at the *Mushroom and Herb Fair* in Rožaje.

SEPTEMBER

Food Fair in Virpazar: wine estates, fruit farmers and bee-keepers present their products. There is dancing and singing.

OCTOBER

Halloween in Budva: witches and elves take over for one day.

DECEMBER

There are free open air *New Year's concerts* in many towns and cities just before midnight on 31 Dec.

PUBLIC HOLIDAYS

1/2 Jan	New Year
6–8 Jan	Orthodox Christmas
17 April 2020, 30 April 2021	
	Orthodox Good Friday
20 April 2020, 3 May 2021	
	Orthodox Easter Monday
1/2 May	Labour Day
21/22 May	Independence Day
13/14 July	National Day

LINKS, BLOGS, APPS & MORE

www.bestof-montenegro.com An excellent resource on Montenegro that offers a great deal of information with numerous categories covering hotels, beaches, restaurants and attractions. The site also has a link to the official tourist site

www.discover-montenegro.com Information on the culture and history, geography and nature. Also tips for activities as well as many photos

www.visit-montenegro.com All you need to know about your destination at a glance: interactive maps with planning function, a link to a video channel with videos about Montenegro, online booking services and much more

lifeinmontenegro.com A Canadian now living in Montenegro dishes the scoop on where to find the best restaurants and bars, and writes about his recent trips and other local adventures

short.travel/mon2 This website introduces Montenegro routes for motorbike riders. The detailed route maps are also useful for holidaymakers on bicycle tours

short.travel/mon17 "Two Wandering Soles" is the blog title of Katie and Ben from Minnesota. The title's wordplay (on wandering, wondering and soles vs. souls) is already a hint about how creative the two Americans are. They present their personal "Best of Montenegro" – including brilliant photos

thesandyfeet.com/places/europe/montenegro Freya gets around a lot – and she shares her impressions with useful tips and beautiful photographies

go.montenegro.travel A smart website from the National Tourist organisation supplements the main website with information

and large-format photos to offer a sensual introduction to the country. (Tip: the English web pages are the most comprehensive)

www.facebook.com/budva The Facebook site is slightly misleading: although there are pictures of Budva, the photographer presents photos from all of Montenegro. Interesting links and videos are also posted here

VIDEOS

www.montenegro.travel/en/multimedia/video A link to a wide selection of travel documentaries showing impressions of the country including mountain biking, hiking, national parks and many other locations

short.travel/mon3 This private travel video shows impressions of the country and guides you among others to the Bay of Kotor, Lake Skadar and Durmitor and Lovćen National Parks

short.travel/mon5 The film on the Durmitor National Park is part of the Traveline series of travel documentaries. Three clips on the Bay of Kotor, Lake Skadar and the train ride through the Morača Canyon on the way from Bar to Belgrade can also be seen on their YouTube channel

short.travel/mon6 The artist Marina Abramović, who has Montenegrin roots, talks in the video about the Macco project in Cetinje (see p. 19). The film is enthralling and was also shown at the Venice Biennale, but it also offers insights into the Montenegrin psyche and Abramović's family history

APPS

Montenegro Talking The augmented reality App for iOS-, Android- and Windows smartphones is an audio guide of Montenegro. Cultural and historic attractions are introduced with information in English and images

Peaks of the Balkans On the Peaks of the Balkans Trail (see p. 89) in the border triangle of Montenegro, Albania and Kosovo the iOS-App is a helpful companion with its detailed offline maps of the Prokletije region

TRAVEL TIPS

ACCOMMODATION

The days of simply furnished rooms *(sobe)* on the coast have come to an end but are still offered in the mountains. Elegant hotels are now shooting up all along the Adriatic.

Good hotels are expensive, but there is still cheap and pleasant private accommodation. Prices vary widely on the coast: Herceg Novi, Budva and Perast are the most expensive and things start to become cheaper after you leave Petrovac and head towards Ulcinj. The prices often fall by up to 40 per cent in the off peak seasons.

In Montenegro, the booking website *www.booking.com* is also very popular – in particular, private owners with some fantastic apartments and guest rooms only take bookings via this website.

RESPONSIBLE TRAVEL

It doesn't take a lot to be environmentally friendly whilst travelling. Don't just think about your carbon footprint whilst flying to and from your holiday destination but also about how you can protect nature and culture abroad. As a tourist it is especially important to respect nature, look out for local products, cycle instead of driving, save water and much more. If you would like to find out more about eco-tourism please visit: *www.ecotourism.org*

ARRIVAL

From the ferry terminal in Calais (France) you can start by taking the A26 trough France, the A25 through Belgium and Luxembourg or the A16 through Belgium, then cross Germany, Austria, Slovenia and Croatia to get to Montenegro. The drive to Tivat takes about 22 hours. Ferries from Dover to Calais and back run many times a day.

The Channel Tunnel connects the United Kingdom and France. There are train connections between London St Pancras and Paris or Brussels (Belgium). Trains depart from several destinations in Europe for Belgrade; this is the unavoidable stopover before travelling on to Montenegro. You then continue on via Bijelo Polje, Mojkovac, Kolašin and Podgorica to Bar on the Adriatic. The landscape along this route is one of the most impressive in the Balkans.

There is a well developed bus network linking Montenegro to Europe via Dubrovnik or Belgrade.

From the UK, you will have one stop, from the USA one or two. Montenegro Airlines *(www.montenegroairlines.com)* flies to Tivat and Podgorica from several European destinations. Air Serbia *(www. airserbia.com)* serves numerous international destinations from Belgrade with connecting flights to Tivat and Podgorica. It is also possible to fly to Dubrovnik and then take a taxi to Montenegro: the trip to Budva (90 km/55.9 mi) costs around 110 euros, to Herceg Novi (20 km/12.4 mi) around 50 euros. You can hire a car there.

From arrival to weather

Your holiday from start to finish: the most important addresses and information for your trip to Montenegro

BANKS & CREDIT CARDS

The daily limit for withdrawals from a cash dispenser is up to 700 euros, depending on the bank. Hotels and supermarkets accept the standard credit cards but you should ask beforehand in restaurants and small shops.

CAMPING

Camping sites are known as *kampovi* or *auto kampovi*. They are always well equipped. *en.camping.info/camp sites* search 'Montenegro'.

CAR HIRE

International and national car hire agencies have branches in most of the major holiday resorts. Travel agencies will also take care of bookings. Good comparison websites are *www.holidayautos.com* and *www.autoeurope.de.* Hire cars are sometimes available for 20 euros per day or even less.

CLIMATE, WHEN TO GO

In July and Aug when the temperatures on the coast can soar to 40 °C/104 °F (or higher in the valley around Podgorica) it is still a temperate 20 °C/68 °F in the Durmitor Mountains. Winters are mild on the coast and harsh in the mountains. The best months for a beach holiday are May/June and Sept/Oct. The extreme heat and overcrowded beaches in the school holiday months of July and Aug can make a holiday stressful during that period. The water temperature is more than 20 °C/68 °F by June and this can reach 29 °C/84 °F at the

BUDGETING

Ice cream	£0.90/$1.15 for one scoop
Snack	£1.75/$2.30 for a slice of pizza
Coffee	£0.90–1.80/$1.15–2.30 for an espresso
Petrol	£1.19–1.23/$1.57–1.62 for 1 litre of super
Bus ticket	£2.20/$2.90 for a trip from Budva to Petrovac (about 20 km/12.4 mi)
Boat tour	£9–35/$11.50–46.50 for a fish picnic

end of the season. There is a good deal of snow in the mountains between Dec and March and it is even possible to ski in some places in summer.

CONSULATES & EMBASSIES

BRITISH EMBASSY
Ulcinjska 8| Podgorica | tel. +382 20 61 80 10 | gov.uk/world/montenegro

UNITED STATES EMBASSY
Džona Džeksona 2 | Podgorica | tel. +382 020 41 05 00 | me.usembassy.gov

CUSTOMS

It is permitted to bring currency up to an amount of 10,000 euros into or out of the country. You are only allowed to import food for your own consumption and also dried fruit, tea and coffee up to a total weight of 1 kg/2.2 lbs, 2 litres of juice and 5 litres of water. In addition, 2 litres of alcohol up to 22 per cent or 1 litre of spirits over 22 per cent and 200 cigarettes or 50 cigars or 250 g of tobacco can be imported duty free.

DRIVING

National registration papers and driving licenses are recognised in Montenegro. It is obligatory to have a green international insurance card and you will need to show it at the border when you enter the country. Maximum speed limits are: in built up areas 40 km/h/25 mph, on country roads 80 km/h/50 mph, on motorways 100 km/h/62 mph. Vehicles with trailers are not allowed to exceed 80 km/h/50 mph.

The legal alcohol limit for drivers is set at 50 mg/100 ml. You must always switch your headlights on at night. Driving without sturdy footwear is also banned. Traffic fines are heavy in Montenegro: overtake in a tunnel or run a red light and you will lose your license; telephoning in the car – at least 20 euros; driving without wearing a seatbelt – 15 euros. You should contact the police immediately if you have an accident. The emergency service *(tel. 1 98 07)* will provide assistance if you have a breakdown on the road.

The country's first motorway section on a 41 km/24.9 mi route around the capital should be completed by 2020. The coastal road between Herceg Novi and Ulcinj as well as roads from the coast to Podgorica and Cetinje are generally busy in high season. You can therefore expect long delays. The parking fees are high on the coast – up to 15 euros a day – and there is usually no guarantee given for the safety of your car.

EMERGENCY SERVICES

Police tel. 122, fire brigade tel. 123, emergency doctor tel. 124, mountain rescue serive tel. 040 25 60 84.

FOR BOOKWORMS AND FILM BUFFS

Encyclopaedia of the Dead – Danilo Kiš (1935–89) is considered to be one of the most important writers in the Balkans. His parables on life, love and death made him famous and most of his books have been published in English

The Battle of Neretva – This film (1969) is one of the several director Veljko Bulajić made in the 1960s that deals with the struggles of the Yugoslav partisans against the German army in the Second World War. The productions were heavily subsidised by the Yugoslav state. The stars include Orson Welles and Yul Brynner

The Brothers Bloom – Rian Johnson filmed the entertaining comedy-drama (2008), which is set in Montenegro and other locations, starring Rachel Weisz, Mark Ruffalo and Adrien Brody. Not only the beach shots along the Adriatic make you want to see more

The November Man – Okay, Roger Donaldson's 2014 spy thriller is not trailblazing cinema. But the lead actor Pierce Brosnan makes the plot very entertaining. And the best of all: most of the scenes for this movie were filmed in Montenegro

Include the country code +382 if you do not have a Montenegrin SIM card.

HEALTH

There are state-run clinics in almost every town or village, they are marked with a red cross. You will have to pay for any treatment you receive and it is therefore a good idea to have foreign travel health insurance with the option of repatriation. Private clinics have been established in the larger towns. The local tourist office can give you the addresses of local doctors – most of them speak English. The well-stocked pharmacies can provide help for minor mishaps.

IMMIGRATION

Visas are not required for those arriving from the EU, Australia, New Zealand, Canada and the US. An identity card is sufficient if you do not plan to be in the country for longer than 30 days but a passport is required for stays of up to 90 days. Tourists from other countries will need a passport and should check with their travel agents what other requirements need to be fulfilled. In Montenegro, each tourist has to be registered with the police. As a rule, the person who provides your accommodation takes care of this and will ask you for your ID or passport when you check in. Remember to take your registration certificate with you when you leave the country – normally, it is not asked for at the border but just in case!

INFORMATION

NACIONALNA TURISTIČKA ORGANIZACIJA CRNE GORE (NTO)
Marka Miljanova 17 | Podgorica | tel. 077 10 00 01 | 24 hour information telephone 08000 13 00 | www.montenegro.travel

CURRENCY CONVERTER

£	€	€	£
1	1.14	1	0.88
3	3.42	3	2.64
5	5.70	5	4.40
13	14.82	13	11.44
40	45.60	40	35.20
75	85.50	75	66
120	136.80	120	105.60
250	285	250	220
500	570	500	440

$	€	€	$
1	0.86	1	1.16
3	2.58	3	3.48
5	4.30	5	5.80
13	11.18	13	15.08
40	34.40	40	46.40
75	64.50	75	87
120	103.20	120	139.20
250	215	250	290
500	430	500	580
500	35,000	5,000	70

For current exchange rates see www.xe.com

The National Tourist Organisation of Montenegro has branches throughout the country and there are travel agencies in almost every town.

NACIONALNI PARKOVI CRNE GORE
Here you will find information on Montenegro's national parks.
Trg Vojvode Bećir-Bega Osmanagića 16 | Podgorica | tel. 020 60 10 15 | www.nparkovi.me

INTERNET & WI-FI

All hotels have wireless connections – and so do most private accommodation and camping sites. Cafés have notices up if they have a Wi-Fi hotspot and some restaurants and pubs provide internet access. As a rule the larger the town, the better the internet connection. Before you go online with your smartphone, you should first check with your service provider about data roaming charges. It can be very expensive outside the EU.

LANGUAGE

It's best to speak English, although not everyone speaks the language yet. If you can speak Russian then make some polite enquiries: some people don't like it, while others like to speak Russian.

Many road signs only have Cyrillic and not Latin script. You can guess some things. Otherwise, the Sat Nav or friendly locals are helpful.

In the south and north-east of Montenegro, Albanian is a second official language after Montenegrin. The road signs are therefore bilingual, e.g. the town Ulcinj is also called Ulqin.

In your MARCO POLO travel guide, you will often notice the abbreviation Sv. It stands for the Montenegrin forms of the word 'saint', i.e. Sveti (masculine) and Sveta (feminine).

NUDISTS

There are limited options for nude bathing in Montenegro. One of the few nudist beaches is on the island of Ada Bojana near Ulcinj. A small rock is reserved for naturists in Ulcinj itself. The small Nijivce nudist beach is located at the outermost tip of Igalo. Fishing boats take tourists from other resorts to small bays where they can bathe nude. Ask on the site!

WEATHER IN BUDVA

	Jan	Feb	March	April	May	June	July	Aug	Sept	Oct	Nov	Dec
Daytime temperature in °C/°F	3/37	3/37	15/59	18/64	22/72	26/79	29/84	29/84	26/79	22/72	15/59	5/41
Nighttime temperatures in °C/°F	-3/27	-2/28	6/43	10/50	14/57	18/64	20/68	20/68	17/63	13/55	8/46	0/32
Sunshine hours/day	3	4	5	7	9	10	11	11	8	7	4	3
Precipitation days/month	14	13	12	13	14	13	9	9	8	11	14	14
Water temperatures in °C/°F	13/55	13/55	14/57	15/59	17/63	22/72	23/73	25/77	22/72	20/68	18/64	15/59

☀ Sunshine hours/day ☂ Precipitation days/month ≋ Water temperatures in °C/°F

OPENING HOURS

There are no fixed opening hours and some shops and restaurants stay open until midnight in summer. The restaurants in this guidebook are open daily at lunchtime and in the evenings, unless otherwise stated. Many offices close at 4pm. Post offices are open from 7am–8pm on weekdays and sometimes longer during the tourist season.

PHONES & MOBILE PHONES

Three mobile phone providers compete for customers: Telenor (069), m:tel (068) and T-Com (067). The prices per minute are higher than elsewhere in Europe and internet connections are also much more expensive. Pre-paid cards with a Montenegrin number from the kiosk or the supermarket can be useful, if you want to use your phone a lot or surf online. If you prefer to use your mobile with your own card, check with your service provider about roaming charges. Montenegro is still not a member of the EU, so it can be expensive. If you are making a call inland, dial the area code or mobile phone code, which always begins with zero, and then the contact number. If you are making a call from a fixed-line inside the same town, there is no need to use the area code. For calls from your home country to Montenegro and vice versa, dial the international dialling code followed by the area or mobile phone code, but omit the first zero and then dial the contact number. International dialling codes: United Kingdom *0044*, Australia *0061*, Canada and USA *001*, Montenegro *00382*.

PRICES & CURRENCY

Food imports especially now cost almost as much as back home. Regional prod-

ucts are more reasonably priced at the market. Petrol is also expensive. And, prices vary throughout the country: for example, many products are cheaper in Bar than in Budva. As a rule, life in the interior is cheaper than on the coast. The sun loungers you hire on the beaches can also be expensive. It is common to pay around 10 euros per day and you can pay up to 100 euros for a luxurious bed shaded by a canopy on the beach.
Montenegro is not a member of the EU, but has independently introduced the euro. At ATMs you also withdraw euro bank notes.

PUBLIC TRANPORT

An extensive bus network connects all of the major cities with each other including the main destinations on the coast. Tickets can be purchased at the bus terminals *(autobuska stanica)* or from the driver and are very inexpensive when compared with the tariffs in the rest of Europe. The train from Bar to Belgrade makes several stops in Sutomore, Podgorica, Kolašin, Mojkovac and Bijelo Polje every day.

TIME

Montenegro has Central European Time (or Central European Summer Time) and is one hour ahead of GMT.

TIPPING

It is customary to round up small amounts in cafés. However, tourists should leave a tip of 10–15 per cent of bill.

VISITORS' TAX

The visitors' tax is about 2 euros and is generally included in the price of your accommodation.

USEFUL PHRASES MONTENEGRIN

PRONUNCIATION

As a general rule, Montenegrin is pronounced as it is written. Special Montenegrin letters and combinations:

c – ts as in cats; č – ch as in church; ć –ch as in future; đ – j as in jungle; dž – j as in adjacent; j – y as in youth; lj – li as in million; nj – ny as in canyon; š – sh as in ship; ž – s as in pleasure.

All vowels are open and must be clearly voiced regardless of their position. In vowel combinations each vowel is audible, as in petnaest = pet-na-est (fifteen). Similarly, the r which plays the role of the syllable nucleus in certain words, must also be clearly voiced: vrba, krk.

The consonants are always pronounced the same, e.g. the g as in gone is always the hard g.

Abbreviation: *f* = female speaker

IN BRIEF

Yes/No/Maybe	da/ne/možda
Please/Thank you	molim/hvala
Excuse me, please!	Oprostite (Izvinite)!
May I ...?	Da li mogu ...?
Pardon?	Molim?
I would like to .../have you got ...?	Želim .../Da li imate?
How much is ...?	Koliko košta?
I (don't) like this.	To mi se (ne) sviđa.
good/bad	dobro/loše
broken/does't work	nije ispravno
too much/much/little	previše/mnogo/malo
all/nothing	sve/ništa
Help!/Attention!/Caution!	Upomoć!/Pažnja!/Oprez!
ambulance/police/fire brigade	ambulantna kola/policija/vatrogasci
Prohibition/forbidden	zabrana/zabranjeno
danger/dangerous	opasnost/opasno
May I take a photo of you?	Da li smem da Vas fotografišem?

GREETINGS, FAREWELL

Good morning!/afternoon!/ evening!/night!	Dobro jutro!/Dobar dan!/ Dobro veče!/Laku noć!
Hello! / Goodbye!/See you!	Zdravo!/Doviđenja!

Govoriš li crnogorski?

"Do you speak Montenegrin?" This guide will help you to say the basic words and phrases in Montenegrin

Bye!	Zdravo!/Ciao!
My name is ...	Zovem se ...
What's your name?	Kako se zovete/zoveš?
I'm from ...	Dolazim iz ...

DATE & TIME

Monday/Tuesday/Wednesday	ponedjeljak/utorak/srijeda
Thursday/Friday/Saturday	četvrtak/petak/subota
Sunday/holiday/	nedjelja/praznik
today/tomorrow/yesterday	danas/sjutra/juče
hour/minute	sat/minuta
day/night/week/month/year	dan/noć/sedmica/mjesec/godina
What time is it?	Je sati?
It's three o'clock.	Tri sata je.
It's half past three.	Tri i po.
a quarter to four.	petnaest do četiri.
a quarter past four.	četiri i petnaest minuta.

TRAVEL

open/closed	otvoreno/zatvoreno
entrance/exit	ulaz/izlaz
departure/arrival	odlazak/polijetanje / dolazak
toilets/ladies/gentlemen	WC, toalet/žene/muškarci
(no) drinking water	(nije) pijaća voda
Where is ...?/Where are ...?	Gdje je ...?/Gdje su ...?
left/right/straight ahead/back	lijevo/desno/pravo/nazad
close/far	blizu/daleko
bus/tram/underground/taxi (cab)	autobus/tramvaj/metro/taksi
stop/taxi (cab) stand	stajalište/taksi-stanica
parking lot/parking garage	parking/parking garaža
street map/map	plan grada/geografska (auto-)karta
train station/harbour/airport	željeznička stanica/luka/aerodrom
schedule/ticket	red vožnje/biljet, karta
single/return/supplement	jednostavno/tamo i nazad/doplata
train/track/platform	voz/kolosek/peron
I would like to rent ...	Htio (f htjela) bih ... da iznajmim.
a car/a bicycle/a boat	auto/bicikl/čamac
petrol/gas station	benzinska pumpa
petrol/gas/diesel	benzin/dizel
breakdown/repair shop	kvar/automehaničarska radionica

FOOD & DRINK

Could you please book a table for tonight for four?	Molim vas rezervaciju za večeras jedan sto za četiri osobe.
on the terrace/by the window	na terasi/pored prozora
The menu, please.	Jelovnik, (meni) molim.
Could I please have ...?	Molim vas, htio (f htjela) bih ...?
bottle/carafe/glass	bocu/bokal/čašu
knife/fork/spoon	nož/viljušku/kašiku
salt/pepper/sugar/vinegar/oil	so/biber/šećer/sirće/ulje
milk/cream/lemon	mlijeko/skorup/limun
with/without ice	sa/bez leda
sparkling/non-sparkling	gazirana/negazirana
vegetarian/allergy	vegetarijanac (f vegetarijanka)/alergija
May I have the bill, please?	Molim vas, htio (f htjela) bih da platim.
bill/receipt/tip	račun/priznanica/bakšiš

SHOPPING

Where can I find...?	Gdje mogu naći?
I'd like .../I'm looking for ...	Htio (f htjela) bih .../Tražim ...
baker/market/grocery	pekara/pijaca/tržnica
shopping centre/department store	šoping mol/robna kuća
supermarket/newspaper shop/kiosk	supermarket/trafika/kiosk
100 grammes/1 kilo	sto grama/jedan kilogram
expensive/cheap/price	skupo/jetino/cijena
more/less	više/manje
organically grown	organska hrana

ACCOMMODATION

I have booked a room.	Rezervisao sam jednu sobu.
Do you have any ... left?	Da li imate još ...?
single room/double room	jednokrevetnu sobu/dvokrevetnu sobu
breakfast/half board/full board (American plan)	doručak/polupansion/puni pansion
at the front/seafront/lakefront	naprijed/prema moru/prema jezeru
shower/sit-down bath/balcony/terrace	tuš/kupatilo/balkon/terasa
key/room card	ključevi/elektronska karta za sobu
luggage/suitcase/bag	prtljag/kufer/torba

BANKS, MONEY & CREDIT CARDS

bank/ATM/pin code	banka/bankovni automat/lični broj
cash/credit card	keš/kreditna kartica
bill/coin/change	novčanica/metalni novac/kusur

HEALTH

doctor/dentist/paediatrician	ljekar/zubar/dječji ljekar, pedijatar
hospital/emergency clinic/pharmacy	bolnica/urgentni centar/apoteka
fever/pain	groznica/bolovi
diarrhoea/nausea	proliv, dijareja/mučnina
sunburn	opekotine od sunca
inflamed/injured	upala, infekcija/povrijeđen
plaster/bandage	flaster/zavoj
pain reliever/tablet/suppository	analgetik/tableta/čepići

POST, TELECOMMUNICATIONS & MEDIA

stamp/letter/postcard	poštanska marka/pismo/razglednica
I need a landline phone card.	Treba mi jedna telefonska kartica za fiksni telefon.
I'm looking for a prepaid card for my mobile.	Tražim jednu pripejd-karticu za mobilni telefon.
Where can I find internet access?	Gdje ću naći internet-vezu?
internet connection/wi-fi	utičnica za internet/WLAN

LEISURE, SPORTS & BEACH

beach/bathing beach	plaža/kupalište
sunshade/lounger	suncobran/ležaljka
low tide/high tide/current	osjeka/plima/struja
cable car/chair lift	žičara/ski-lift
(rescue) hut/avalanche	planinska brvnara/lavina

NUMBERS

0	nula	15	petnaest
1	jedan (f jedna, n jedno)	16	šesnaest
2	dva (f dvije)	17	sedamnaest
3	tri	18	osamnaest
4	četiri	19	devetnaest
5	pet	70	sedamdeset
6	šest	80	osamdeset
7	sedam	90	devedeset
8	osam	100	sto, stotina
9	devet	200	dvjesta
10	deset	1000	hiljadu
11	jedanaest	2000	dvije hiljade
12	dvanaest	10000	deset hiljada
13	trinaest	½	polovina
14	četrnaest	¼	četvrtina

ROAD ATLAS

Exploring Montenegro

The map on the back cover shows how the area has been sub-divided

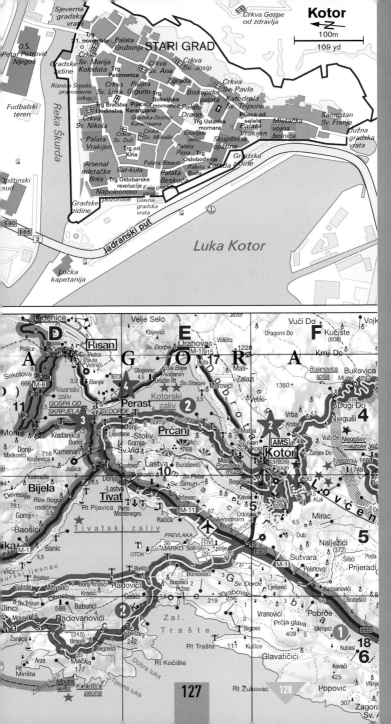

Zabljak

A Berslavci (24)
Bijelo Polje
B **C**

129
Kurilo
Plavnica

1 *Jadranska*
magistrala
Nacionalni

52 M-2
Man. Sv. Nikola
park

Vranjina
302 129

Lesendra
Malo
blato
9

Dobovica
Skadarsko jezero

2 GRMOŽUR
Raduš Krnjice
Krnjičko oko
Skadarsko jezer

ahovo Zabes
Seoca
4
STARČEVO

Bolievici 510
Godinje
Vučedapici
Dračevica
Duravci

3
Golik
Karanikíci
Sestani
Sv. Dorde
BEŠKA

Pepici
Dedíci
Donj
Beš
(107)
MORAČNI

3 Limljani
425
933
Dedíci
Murići
Bobovištans
Bijaca

Tunel Sozina
Gornji
kraj
Selijevica
1028
Gurza
Gornji-
Pinčíci
5.5
Livari
Gornja-
707
Tejan

1160
1186
Tudemili
(364)
978
Briska
Donja-
5.5

884
Sutorman
8.5
a
m

1
Sv. Nikola 1182
Zupci
Rumija
1593
Lumetić
i

Tekia
Dumani
Papani
Zánkovici
Mali
Mikulíci
1174-G
Medu

S Dumani
Sv. Dimitrije
685
Sustas
2.5
C R N A (**M O N T E N E G R O**)

M-1
Haj Nehaj
Madžari
Brca
Šušanj
(145)
2.5
Veliki
Mikulíci

aligrad 232 Sutomore
496 Zagrab
4 260
9
Stari Bar
Bartula
Loška
1351
Knježdevo
Dabe

Sutomorski
zaliv
Čatuna
Tomba
Mahala
Lisíce
Velje Selo (468)

Boškovićeva kula
Crni rt
Barsko
Topolica
sidrište
Zaljev
Poda
Dobra
Voda
4

Volujlca
Bar AMS
Voluvica
M-1
Mrk
Pecurie
Komina 2
(32

5 Veliki Zabio
256
7.5
4
Mrkojević
Dubrava
Rt Maret
Kunje
Kárastani

Masline
23
Kruče

Staro Ulcinj
Kruče

Jadransko More
Rt Rep

6
4 km
2.49 mi
Valda
Rt Mendra

KEY TO ROAD ATLAS

German	Symbol	English
Autobahn · Gebührenpflichtige Anschlussstelle · Gebührenstelle · Anschlussstelle mit Nummer · Rasthaus mit Übernachtung · Raststätte · Kleinraststätte · Tankstelle · Parkplatz mit und ohne WC	Trento	Motorway · Toll junction · Toll station · Junction with number · Motel · Restaurant · Snackbar · Filling-station · Parking place with and without WC
Autobahn in Bau und geplant mit Datum der voraussichtlichen Verkehrsübergabe	Datum Date	Motorway under construction and projected with expected date of opening
Zwoibahnige Straße (4-spurig)		Dual carriageway (4 lanes)
Fernverkehrsstraße · Straßennummern	14 E45	Trunk road · Road numbers
Wichtige Hauptstraße		Important main road
Hauptstraße · Tunnel · Brücke	)==(	Main road · Tunnel · Bridge
Nebenstraßen		Minor roads
Fahrweg · Fußweg		Track · Footpath
Wanderweg (Auswahl)		Tourist footpath (selection)
Eisenbahn mit Fernverkehr		Main line railway
Zahnradbahn, Standseilbahn		Rack-railway, funicular
Kabinenschwebebahn · Sessellift		Aerial cableway · Chair-lift
Autofähre · Personenfähre		Car ferry · Passenger ferry
Schifffahrtslinie		Shipping route
Naturschutzgebiet · Sperrgebiet		Nature reserve · Prohibited area
Nationalpark · Naturpark · Wald		National park · natural park · Forest
Straße für Kfz. gesperrt	X X X X X	Road closed to motor vehicles
Straße mit Gebühr		Toll road
Straße mit Wintersperre	XII-II	Road closed in winter
Straße für Wohnanhänger gesperrt bzw. nicht empfehlenswert		Road closed or not recommended for caravans
Touristenstraße · Pass	Weinstraße 1510	Tourist route · Pass
Schöner Ausblick · Rundblick · Landschaftlich bes. schöne Strecke		Scenic view · Panoramic view · Route with beautiful scenery
Heilbad · Schwimmbad		Spa · Swimming pool
Jugendherberge · Campingplatz	X X	Youth hostel · Camping site
Golfplatz · Sprungschanze		Golf-course · Ski jump
Kirche im Ort, freistehend · Kapelle		Church · Chapel
Kloster · Klosterruine		Monastery · Monastery ruin
Synagoge · Moschee		Synagogue · Mosque
Schloss, Burg · Schloss-, Burgruine		Palace, castle · Ruin
Turm · Funk-, Fernsehturm		Tower · Radio-, TV-tower
Leuchtturm · Kraftwerk		Lighthouse · Power station
Wasserfall · Schleuse		Waterfall · Lock
Bauwerk · Marktplatz, Areal		Important building · Market place, area
Ausgrabungs- u. Ruinenstätte · Bergwerk		Arch. excavation, ruins · Mine
Dolmen · Menhir · Nuraghen	π	Dolmen · Menhir · Nuraghe
Hünen-, Hügelgrab · Soldatenfriedhof		Cairn · Military cemetery
Hotel, Gasthaus, Berghütte · Höhle		Hotel, inn, refuge · Cave

Kultur
Culture

Malerisches Ortsbild · Ortshöhe	WIEN (171)	Picturesque town · Elevation
Eine Reise wert	★★ MILANO	Worth a journey
Lohnt einen Umweg	★ TEMPLIN	Worth a detour
Sehenswert	Andermatt	Worth seeing

Landschaft
Landscape

Eine Reise wert	★★ Las Cañadas	Worth a journey
Lohnt einen Umweg	★ Texel	Worth a detour
Sehenswert	Dikti	Worth seeing

MARCO POLO Erlebnistour 1		**MARCO POLO Discovery Tour 1**
MARCO POLO Erlebnistouren		**MARCO POLO Discovery Tours**
MARCO POLO Highlight	★1	**MARCO POLO Highlight**

MARCO POLO TRAVEL GUIDES

Travel with
Insider
Tips

INDEX

This index lists all places, destinations, mountains, rivers and persons featured in this guide. Numbers in bold indicate a main entry.

WRITE TO US

e-mail: info@marcopologuides.co.uk
Did you have a great holiday?
Is there something on your mind?
Whatever it is, let us know!
Whether you want to praise, alert us
to errors or give us a personal tip –
MARCO POLO would be pleased to
hear from you.
We do everything we can to provide the
very latest information for your trip.

Nevertheless, despite all of our authors'
thorough research, errors can creep in.
MARCO POLO does not accept any
liability for this. Please contact us by
e-mail or post.
MARCO POLO Travel Publishing Ltd
Pinewood, Chineham Business Park
Crockford Lane, Chineham
Basingstoke, Hampshire RG24 8AL
United Kingdom

PICTURE CREDITS
Cover photograph: St Nicholas Church, Perast, Kotor Bay (Schapowalow/4Corners: J. Foulkes)
Photos: R. Freyer (14/15), Gelly Images: E. Börner (107), B. Brecelj (19 bottom), S. Condrea (23), L. L. Grand-adam (4 bottom, 28 right), Istankov (68), O. Slobodeniuk (2); Getty Images/MStudioImages (5, 102/103); huber-images: Grandadam (28 left), J. Huber (12/13, 50, 59), S. Kremer (41, 110 bottom), B. Morandi (20/21), S. Surac (74); G. Knoll (61, 106/107); Laif: M. Cavalier (26/27, 73), Henseler (43), K. Henseler (4 top 32/33), F. Heuer (flap left, 11, 17, 29, 44, 81, 82, 89, 104, 111), T. & B. Morandi (52, 70, 122/123), Zahn (9); Laif/Haytham-Rea: L Cousin (37); Laif/Le Figaro Magazine: E. Martin (7, 56); Laif/NYT/Redux: C. Chase (18 centre); Laif/robertharding: S. Black (63), A. Copson (31, 64/65), F. Fell (30/31, 55, 95); Lookphotos: G. Bayerl (48/49, 110 top), D. Schoenen (47); Lookphotos/Blend Images (18 top); Lookphotos/robertharding (90/91); mauritius images/agefotostock: S. Hauser (108/109), K. Zelazowski (38); mauritius images/Alamy (8, 78), eFesenko (34), B. Klement (97), E. Lokteva (19 top); mauritius images/Aurora RF: M. Radovanovic (24); mauritius images/image anorak/Alamy (18 bottom); mauritius images/imagebroker (86, C. Handl (76/77); mauritius images/imagebroker/Paul Williams - Funkystock (flap right); mauritius images/Lumi Images: Romulic-Stojcic (108), D. Secen (3); mauritius images/Prisma: S. Ember (30); mauritius images/RnDmS/Alamy (10, 84/85); mauritius images/Westend61: E. Strigl (6, 66); mauritius images/Zoonar/Alamy (101); C. Nowak (109); Schapowalow/4Corners: J. Foulkes (1); Transit Archiv: Rotting (106)

3rd edition 2020 – fully revised and updated
Worldwide Distribution: Marco Polo Travel Publishing Ltd, Pinewood, Chineham
Business Park, Crockford Lane, Basingstoke, Hampshire RG 24 8AL, United Kingdom. Email: sales@marcopolouk.com
© MAIRDUMONT GmbH & Co. KG, Ostfildern
Authors: Mirko Kaupat, Danja Antonović
Editor: Felix Wolf
Picture editor: Veronika Plajer
Cartography road atlas: © MAIRDUMONT, Ostfildern; cartography pull-out map: © MAIRDUMONT, Ostfildern
Cover design, p. 1, pull-out map cover: Karl Anders – Studio für Brand Profiling, Hamburg; design inside:
milchhof:atelier, Berlin; design p. 2/3, Discovery Tours: Susan Chaaban Dipl.-Des. (FH)
Translated from German by Robert Scott McInnes and Dr. Suzanne Kirkbright
Editorial office: SAW Communications, Redaktionsbüro Dr. Sabine A. Werner, Mainz: Julia Gilcher, Cosima Talhouni, Dr. Sabine A. Werner; Prepress: SAW Communications, Mainz, in cooperation with alles mit Medien, Mainz
Phrase book in cooperation with Ernst Klett Sprachen GmbH, Stuttgart,
Editorial by PONS Wörterbücher

MIX
Paper from
responsible sources
FSC® C124385

DOS & DON'TS ✊

Here are a few things you should look out for in Montenegro

DO OBEY THE SPEED LIMIT

It can be annoying when buses and trucks hold up traffic and you are forced to putter along behind them. If this happens, don't be tempted to step on the accelerator rather try to relax and drive slowly and carefully, a safer option on the winding roads in the mountains of Montenegro. And, there are radar traps and police everywhere to make sure you adhere to the speed limit.

DON'T WEAR SHOES IN MOSQUES

Spontaneous invitations to visit the mosque are quite common in small Muslim communities. Do what the Muslims do and remove your shoes before you enter! If you visit a church or monastery, make sure you are not too casually dressed. By the way, members of the Orthodox faith leave religious places backwards – with their eyes fixed on the icons.

DO FIRST AGREE ON A RATE FOR YOUR TAXI

There are plenty of taxis – especially in the resort towns on the coast – but not all of the drivers are honest. A taxi meter plays no role, the price you agree on before you set out is the real charge so before you get into a taxi you must negotiate the fare. Most of the drivers speak a smattering of English. Take care that you are travelling in a registered taxi with an official number and not a private taxi.

DON'T UNDERESTIMATE THE BLACK MOUNTAIN

The mountainous north is still something of an insiders' tip. But the weather can be unpredictable at an altitude of 1,500 m/4,921 ft, and the paths are not always that well marked. This makes it a good idea go on hikes in groups of at least three and take a mountain guide with you. Always check the weather report before you set out and make sure you let the people you are staying with know where you are going. And, just to be sure, take the telephone number of your hotel with you.

DON'T DRINK TAP WATER

Every year the drinking water is improving. But so-called 'technical water' still comes out of the tap. You should not drink it – if in doubt, always ask beforehand.

DON'T ASK QUESTIONS ABOUT LANGUAGE AND RELIGION

Montenegro is a multicultural country: Serbs, Albanians, Croatians and Bosnians live here – less than half of the population consider themselves Montenegrins. The situation is complicated and disagreements over language and nation continue. The question of religion is no less complicated. If you get into a conversation with one of the locals, it's best to tackle these subjects politely.